THE FATE OF THE NINTH

Carlisle
EBURACUM
CALLEVA
Nijmegen
ANCONA
ROMA
MINTURNAE
ELEGEIA
LAMBAESIS
PETRA

DUNCAN B. CAMPBELL

THE FATE OF THE NINTH

The curious disappearance of one of Rome's legions

Bocca della Verità Publishing
Glasgow

Copyright © 2018 by Duncan B Campbell.
The right of Duncan B Campbell to be identified as the author of this work has been asserted in accordance with the Copyright, Designs and Patents Act 1988.

All rights reserved. No part of this book may be reprinted or reproduced or utilized in any form or by any electronic, mechanical or other means, now known or hereafter invented, including photocopying or recording, or in any information storage and retrieval systems, without permission in writing from the author. The only exception is by a reviewer, who may quote short excerpts in a review.

Cover designed by Bocca della Verità Publishing

This book is a work of historical research. Names, characters, places, and incidents are products of the author's research. Any resemblance to actual persons, living or dead, events, or locales is entirely intentional.

Second Printing: 2019
Bocca della Verità Publishing

ISBN-13 978-1-791-76833-1

Independently published through Amazon

*For Harrison,
in the hope that it will not spoil his
enjoyment of the adventures of
Marcus Flavius Aquila*

AUTHOR'S PREFACE

As a child, one of the first books I owned – and returned to, again and again – was *Julius Caesar and Roman Britain*, a Ladybird "Adventure from History" book, illustrated by the excellent John T. Kenney, perhaps better known as the original Thomas the Tank Engine illustrator. (Why do we always remember the illustrator?) It was from this book that I first learned that, under the emperor Hadrian, "the two great tribes north and south of the Scottish border had risen in revolt and slaughtered the whole of the officers and men of the IX Legion, stationed at York".

Naturally, Rosemary Sutcliff's *The Eagle of the Ninth* became another of my favourite books, based as it was on the premise of an accursed legion sent north from Eburacum to quell the rebellious Caledonians, at whose hands it finally suffered annihilation, shrunken by desertion and disgraced by mutiny. I well remember thrilling to the BBC TV adaptation in 1977, with its replica of the Silchester eagle as its centrepiece.

The story has captivated successive generations, while the 2010 motion picture *The Eagle* encouraged renewed interest in the Ninth Legion. However, although researchers have long known that Sutcliff's story was based upon an erroneous version of events, the basis of their knowledge has often been entirely misunderstood and, for that reason, equally often rejected. It is the humble purpose of this little book to marshal the known facts in one place and to explain their significance, so that readers will be better equipped to decide the issue for themselves.

A NOTE ON THE FOOTNOTES

I love footnotes. They sit unobtrusively at the bottom of the page, waiting to provide bibliographic details for those who might wish to pursue a particular avenue of research or check the veracity of a particular statement. Those who simply wish to read the narrative should feel free to ignore them entirely, in the secure knowledge that they are not missing anything.

D.B.C.
Glasgow, November 2018

CONTENTS

Author's Preface vii

List of illustrations xi

Introduction 1

1 A Very Interesting Stone 19

2 A Phantom Tile 27

3 One of Our Legions is Missing 36

4 The Man from Minturno 50

5 The Finest Tomb in Petra 61

6 The Patron of Timgad 70

7 Picts, Scots, and Brigantes 81

8 The Broken Eagle 89

9 In Mommsen's Shadow 101

10 An Unnecessary War 111

11 Taking the Waters 119

12 The Consul of AD 161 132

Epilogue 140

Timeline of Emperors 145

Index 147

x

LIST OF ILLUSTRATIONS

Figure 1: Tombstone of Rufinus from York 18

Figure 2: The "very interesting Roman stone" from York 21

Figure 3: Boissard's version of Laelianus' statue base 29

Figure 4: Roofing tile (tegula) of the Ninth Legion 33

Figure 5: Tombstone of Flavinus from Lincoln. 41

Figure 6: Boissard's sketch of the legionary pillar 48

Figure 7: Career inscription of Burbuleius 52

Figure 8: Tomb of Florentinus in Petra 63

Figure 9: Dedication by Crispinus at Lambaesis 76

Figure 10: The Silchester eagle 95

Figure 11: Hadrian's titulature on the coinage 104

Figure 12: Two fragments of tile from Nijmegen 122

INTRODUCTION

THE "FATE OF THE NINTH" is a story told through Roman inscriptions. Of course, the work of Roman authors like Tacitus and Cassius Dio is often relevant, as are the findings of archaeology; but the main facts, such as they are, have been gleaned chiefly from inscriptions. So, a few words about epigraphy are necessary.

Epigraphy is the study of ancient inscribed texts, chiefly, but not exclusively, those carved onto stone. It has frequently been observed that the ancient Romans had "the epigraphic habit", a phrase coined in 1982 by the American scholar Ramsay MacMullen for a phenomenon that had been recognized for centuries: namely, the predilection of the Romans to record various events for posterity, whether it was (in MacMullen's words) "a life ended, a vow made, or an honour voted".[1]

The Roman army were amongst the most prolific generators of inscriptions, from the tombstones that listed a man's military career to the building inscriptions that recorded the erection of some archaeologically identifiable structure.

---

[1] R. MacMullen, "The epigraphic habit in the Roman empire", *American Journal of Philology* Vol. 103 (1982), pp. 233-246.

Roman epitaphs, dedications, honorary texts, and administrative decrees abound. As an added bonus, military building inscriptions generally invoked the reigning emperor, either by expressing allegiance to him or by acknowledging his responsibility for the work done on his behalf. This is important because the erection of the inscription can often be closely dated by the combination of titles or offices held by the emperor during a particular period of time. Most useful, in this respect, is the *tribunicia potestas* ("tribunician power"), which had to be renewed annually, normally on 10 December, in order to ensure that the emperor benefitted from the traditional powers of the tribune, including his sacrosanctity.

Antiquarians and travellers had always been intrigued by Roman inscriptions and duly recorded them as curiosities. Their systematic study was greatly assisted by the publication, in 1603, of the Flemish scholar Jan Gruter's compendium of more than 10,000 examples, re-issued a century later in a new edition by the German Johann Georg Graevius.[2] In the meantime, the Italian scholar Raffaele Fabretti had published his own collection, offering some corrections to Gruter's texts.[3] Later generations could also consult the more extensive two-volume collection published by the Swiss scholar Johann

---

[2] J. Gruter, *Inscriptiones antiquae totius orbis Romani, in corpus absolutissimum redactae* (Heidelberg 1603; 2nd edn. Amsterdam 1707).

[3] R. Fabretti, *Inscriptionum antiquarum quae in aedibus paternis asservantur explicatio et additamentum* (Rome 1699).

Caspar von Orelli, with supplementary third volume contributed by the German archaeologist Wilhelm Henzen.[4]

The nineteenth century saw a burgeoning of interest, culminating in the creation of the *Corpus Inscriptionum Latinarum* project (known as *CIL*) in the 1850s.[5] Its goal was to collect and publish all of the inscriptions that survived from the Roman empire in a series of folio-sized volumes arranged by geographical region, and its driving force was the scholar Theodor Mommsen, who believed that only by organizing inscriptions in this way would they become useful. While Mommsen himself tackled eastern Europe and northern Italy, producing (for the former) *CIL* III in 1873 and (for the latter) *CIL* V in 1872, other areas were assigned to suitably qualified colleagues. For example, the inscriptions of north Africa, collected by Mommsen's student Gustav Wilmanns, were published in 1881, after his tragically early death, as *CIL* VIII, while responsibility for the inscriptions of Spain and Britain was handed over to Emil Hübner, who duly published (for the former) *CIL* II in 1869 and (for the latter) *CIL* VII in 1873. Of course, the discovery of new inscriptions continued apace, necessitating supplementary volumes right up to the present day, and while Wilmanns had produced his own collection of

---

[4] J.C. Orellius, *Inscriptionum Latinarum selectarum amplissima collectio ad illustrandam Romanae antiquitatis disciplinam accommodata*, 2 vols. (Zurich 1828); vol. 3 (Zurich 1856).

[5] The first fruits of the project appeared in 1863: Th. Mommsen, *Corpus Inscriptionum Latinarum* Vol. 1: *Inscriptiones Latinae Antiquissimae ad C. Caesaris mortem* (Berlin 1863).

texts in the style of Gruter and Orelli,[6] it was not widely used, and it is the multi-volume compendium of Hermann Dessau that has stood the test of time.[7]

In the case of Britain, events took a different turn, and from the 1920s, rather than contributing to *CIL*, British scholars made their own arrangements, culminating in *The Roman Inscriptions of Britain* (*RIB*), the first volume of which appeared in 1965. Meanwhile, in 1889, the French epigraphist René Cagnat had begun gathering each year's epigraphic discoveries from around the Roman empire and reporting them in *L'anneé épigraphique* (*AE*), a publication of the Presses Universitaires de France. Thus, the inscriptions mentioned in this book will be identified either by a "CIL" number, an "RIB" number, or an "AE" number.

The twentieth century has seen the gradual increase, year by year, in the sheer volume of published inscriptions. For example, while the 1900 edition of *L'année épigraphique* registered only 224 items, the 2000 edition carried 1,869. The twenty-first century seems to be witnessing a corresponding increase in the reporting of so-called diplomas – the twin-leaved bronze documents issued to certain time-served veterans as incontrovertible proof of their legal status as Roman citizens – either as complete surviving examples or, more commonly, as fragments. Where the 2000 edition of *L'année*

---

[6] G. Wilmanns, *Exempla Inscriptionum Latinarum in usum praecipue academicum*, 2 vols. (Berlin 1873).

[7] H. Dessau, *Inscriptiones Latinae Selectae*, 5 vols. (Berlin 1892-1916).

épigraphique registered only four, the 2009 edition carried fully 46 of these. The cumulative benefits for epigraphers and military historians are incalculable. Where a reasonably complete text can be recovered, such a document offers the hope, not only of a list of military units in a given province discharging veterans on the same day, but also of the names of the recipient and his commanding officer, the provincial governor, and the consuls who were serving in Rome on that precise date. The importance of this last aspect will become clear in the course of this book.

✳ ✳ ✳

The "Fate of the Ninth" is also a story about Roman legions, so a few words on the Roman army are appropriate here. The army was fully integrated into Roman society. Provincials could enlist in the auxiliary regiments, the 500- or 1000-strong *cohortes* of infantry and *alae* of cavalry, and on their retirement after 26 years of service, they were granted the much-coveted Roman citizenship and the right to marry legally (as stated in the text of their diploma). The fortified bases where they served, designated as "forts" by modern scholars, were mostly strung out along the frontiers of the empire or in the hinterland, linked by the famous road network of the Roman empire.

Roman citizens, on the other hand, could enlist as legionaries and serve for 25 or 26 years (veterans appear to have been discharged only every second year), enjoying the benefits of regular pay and medical care in the relatively hygienic and orderly surroundings of a legionary fortress. Far fewer than the forts of the auxiliaries, they were also far larger, designed to accommodate the 5000 or so men of a legion. At a time when the quarrymen in Egypt, for example, were paid 47 sesterces per month,[8] many will have preferred the legionary's guaranteed annual salary of 1,200 sesterces. The only disadvantage was the possibility of death on a battlefield. But for those with moderate education, there was the option of advancement to a more comfortable position in a records office or on the staff of a senior officer, while there was an outside chance of promotion into the highly prestigious (and well paid) legionary centurionate, otherwise populated by time-served Praetorians and the sons of municipal families.

The importance of the centurions stemmed from their role as career soldiers, often moving from legion to legion in an endeavour to rise, via an as-yet poorly understood hierarchy, to the key position of *primus pilus* ("chief centurion"), in charge of the other 59 centurions of the legion. By then, a man might be around 50 years of age, if he had risen through the ranks, but his completion of the one-year stint as *primus pilus* gave him new status as a *primipilaris*, which qualified him either to serve at the emperor's pleasure in some special command, or to remain with his legion as *praefectus castrorum*

---

[8] H. Cuvigny, "The amount of wages paid to the quarry-workers at Mons Claudianus", *Journal of Roman Studies* Vol. 86 (1996), pp. 139-145.

("prefect of the camp"), where he was effectively the most experienced soldier.

By contrast, the high military commands were only brief stages in an aristocrat's political career. While the auxiliary regiments were commanded by men belonging to the elite *ordo equester*, or equestrian order, the officers of the legions were mostly senators. The difference was chiefly one of wealth.

The emperor Augustus had decided that the senate should comprise around 600 men who possessed property to the value of one million sesterces. Every year, there were twenty new entrants, who were elected to the post of *quaestor* (a kind of financial assistant) at the age of 25; ten of them were assigned by lot to assist the proconsuls of the senatorial provinces,[9] and the others remained in Rome, where some were attached to the consuls and others to the emperor. All had previously served, in their teenage years, on one of the four boards of minor magistracies that made up the vigintivirate ("college of twenty men"), and all, by and large, would progress to the largely honorific post of *tribunus plebis* ("tribune of the plebs"). Their number appears to have been sufficient, broadly speaking, to compensate for the natural wastage in the senate brought about by old age and disease in the notoriously unhealthy climate of Rome.

---

[9] The ten provinces within the senate's purview comprised the consular provinces of Asia and Africa, and the praetorian provinces of Achaia, Creta-Cyrene, Cyprus, Gallia Narbonensis, Hispania Baetica, Macedonia, Pontus-Bithynia, and Sicilia.

To advance their career, senators were obliged to follow a strictly defined sequence of offices, known as the *cursus honorum*, observing the minimum age for each one. Thus, a man could not hold the praetorship until the age of 29, except that, under the terms of the *ius liberorum* ("right to the privileges of those with children"), introduced to encourage the growth of senatorial families, "a year is remitted for every child", which (for example) enabled the 27-year-old Agricola to hold the praetorship in AD 68 on account of his two children.[10] This particular office, available to 18 men each year, opened up a range of posts of praetorian rank; these included the prefecture of one of the three treasuries at Rome, the command of a legion as *legatus legionis*, and the governorship of a praetorian province (broadly speaking, those without a legionary garrison), either as *legatus Augusti pro praetore* (for those in the emperor's portion) or as *proconsul* (for those in the senate's portion).[11] While the proconsulates were renewed annually, scholars have estimated that the imperial commands had an average tenure of three years.

The ultimate goal for all senators was the consulship, traditionally limited to those aged at least 41, though this was

---

[10] *Digest of Roman Law* 4.4.2: ... *singuli anni per singulos liberos remittantur*. For Agricola's praetorship, see Tac., *Agr.* 6.4.

[11] On the accession of Hadrian, the praetorian imperial provinces were Arabia, Cilicia, Galatia, Gallia Aquitania, Gallia Belgica, Gallia Lugdunensis, Judaea (until Hadrian replaced it with Dacia superior), Lusitania, Lycia-Pamphylia, Pannonia inferior, Thracia, and the command of the Third Augusta Legion in the territory of Numidia. See *supra*, n. 9, for the praetorian senatorial provinces.

again mitigated by the workings of the *ius liberorum*. It was the emperor Trajan's grant of the *ius trium liberorum* ("right to the privileges of those with three children") that qualified the childless Pliny the Younger to hold the consulship in AD 100, when aged only 39.[12]

Each year, the two *consules ordinarii* ("consuls elected in the usual manner") traditionally stepped down at some point to enable successive pairs of colleagues to become *consules suffecti* ("substitute consuls"). With an average of eight men holding the consulship each year, it is clear that only around half of all senators could be honoured in this way. But only thus could a man qualify for posts of consular rank, which included the *praefectus urbi* (Prefect of the City of Rome), the *curator aquarum* (Curator of the water supply), and (perhaps most importantly) the governorship of provinces that held a legionary garrison.[13] The prestigious one-year proconsulships of Asia and Africa were likewise the preserve of these so-called consulars and normally formed the pinnacle of their career, when aged around 50.

By contrast with the 600-strong *ordo senatorius*, the equestrian order had perhaps thirty or forty times as many members, no doubt owing to the lower property qualification of

---

[12] Pliny, *Letters* 10.2. See also *infra*, pp. 22-23 on the consulship.

[13] On the accession of Hadrian, the consular imperial provinces were Britannia, Cappadocia, Dacia (until Hadrian replaced it with Judaea, now renamed Syria Palaestina), Dalmatia (though long bereft of legions), Germania inferior, Germania superior, Hispania Tarraconensis, Moesia inferior, Moesia superior, Pannonia superior, and Syria.

400,000 sesterces. Like senators, many *equites* were rich landowners, though equally many derived their wealth from entrepreneurial activities and served their communities by holding civic magistracies.

Unlike the senatorial *cursus honorum*, there was no requirement for *equites* to perform public service. Nevertheless, many chose to enter the *militia equestris* ("equestrian military service"), perhaps after having held civic office as a town decurion at the age of around 30. The standard sequence of posts led from the command of an infantry cohort as its prefect, through service as an equestrian tribune on the staff of a legionary commander, to the command of an *ala* (cavalry squadron). Successful completion might lead on to a lucrative administrative post as a provincial procurator, and for an ambitious few, to the three great prefectures: the *praefectus annonae* in charge of the grain supply at Rome, the *praefectus Aegypti* governing the important province of Egypt, and, most prestigious of all, the *praefectus praetorio* commanding the Praetorian Guard.

✶ ✶ ✶

It is the centuries-long study of inscriptions that underpins our understanding of the Roman army and the respective roles played by senators and equestrians in commanding it, and by the ordinary inhabitants of the empire in manning it. The findspots of these inscriptions can often shed light on the movements of the military units that they mention. And it is largely the interpretation of particular men's careers, as set out on inscriptions, that has helped to illuminate the history of the Ninth Legion, for wherever the dating of one stage in a man's career can be ascertained, it is often possible to suggest the dating of the other stages, however tentatively.

As will be seen, the argument often turns upon a particular man's posting as *tribunus laticlavius*, or "broad-striped tribune", in reference to the senator's prerogative of wearing a broad purple stripe on his tunic. Unfortunately, the rules that governed the holding of this post remain obscure. It is clear that it was held prior to a man's entry to the senate, but after his vigintivirate. Thus, we might envisage a tribune of around nineteen or twenty years of age, like Agricola when he served with one of the legions of Britain during the Boudiccan revolt of AD 60,[14] or a few years older, like Quintus Sicinius Maximus, a former *decemvir stlitibus iudicandis* (one of ten minor magistrates connected with the judicial courts), who died at the age of 23, while serving as tribune in the Fourth Flavia Felix Legion.[15]

Dating a man's tribunate is further complicated by the realization that the post cannot normally have been of twelve months' duration, if all thirty legions were to have one, and in fact, tenure may normally have been for two or three years, as not all *vigintiviri* appear to have held the post. Referring to Agricola's tribunate, Tacitus records that he "won approval

---

[14] Tac., *Agr.* 5.1 for his tribunate, and *Agr.* 44.1 for his birth date of 13 June AD 40. See *infra*, p. 40, for the Boudiccan revolt.
[15] *AE* 1913, 172.

for this first stint of soldiering from Suetonius Paullinus, a diligent and circumspect commander, having been selected for assessment as his tent companion",[16] which perhaps suggests that, even if he hadn't arrived with Paullinus in AD 58, he may have remained in post until Paullinus' departure in summer AD 61.

We may imagine a similarly extended tenure for Gaius Vesnius Vindex. Having been *quattuorvir viarum curandarum* (one of four minor magistrates concerned with maintaining the streets of Rome), he found himself tribune of the Eighth Augusta Legion during the "deserters' war" of AD 186-187, "when the pious and faithful legion was relieved from a blockade and was named steadfast and Commodan",[17] for showing loyalty to the emperor Commodus in time of danger.[18] The inscription celebrating Vindex's career indicates that he was rewarded by being designated for the quaestorship at the age of 23, thus at least a year early.

In addition, a handful of men are known to have served as *tribunus laticlavius* in more than one legion, thus reducing the opportunities open to their peers. In order to complete two or three tours of duty, they perhaps simply started earlier and moved straight into their quaestorship. Lucius Minicius Natalis Quadronius Verus, whose role as *triumvir monetalis auro argento aere flando feriundo* (one of the three holders of the

---

[16] Tac., *Agr.* 5.1.//
[17] *CIL* XI, 6053.//
[18] For the war, see Herodian, *History of the Roman Empire* 1.10.1-7.

highly coveted magistracy in charge of the imperial mint) marked him out for a promising career, was tribune of the First Adiutrix Legion, the Eleventh Claudia Legion, and the Fourteenth Gemina Legion in succession, before entering the senate as a candidate of the emperor Hadrian,[19] while the spectacularly polyonymous Salvius Nenolaus Campanianus Gnaeus Plotius Maximinus Titus Hoenius Severus Serveienus Ursus, a former *triumvir capitalis* (one of the three holders of the less coveted magistracy concerned with criminal jurisdiction), held tribunates in the Fifth Macedonica Legion and the First Adiutrix Legion before dying at the age of 21 years, nine months, and 3 days.[20]

Thus, when we meet such senatorial tribunes in the course of this book, we may envisage young men of around 20 years of age.

It is often stated that the *tribunus laticlavius* was the second-in-command of a legion, although the wisdom of placing an inexperienced youth in command of 5,000 fighting men seems never to have been questioned, far less the absurdity of obliging the seasoned *praefectus castrorum* to defer to his judgement. Moreover, it has equally often been assumed that the *tribunus laticlavius* was the only officer authorized to lead a battle-group of legionary *vexillarii* ("detached soldiers"). Both theories originated in the work of the German scholar Alfred von Domaszewski, and each one is worth examining.

---

[19] *CIL* II, 4509 = 6145 = *ILS* 1029; XIV, 3599 = *ILS* 1061.
[20] *CIL* III, 6755.

Firstly, a fragmentary inscription discovered in 1881 at Lambaesis, fortress of the Third Augusta Legion in present-day Algeria, demonstrated the tribune's relative seniority to Domaszewski's satisfaction.[21] After a preliminary dedication to an imperial personage (apparently Septimius Severus' ill-starred son Geta, which would account for the wanton damage that the stone has suffered),[22] the stone carries the heading *TRIB[--]* (the right-hand side of the inscription is entirely lost) followed by a list of names, only the first three of which survive with any reasonable legibility (although traces of a fourth can be discerned). These are Flavius Balbus (whose name is followed by a word beginning with L), Teltonius Marcellus, and Licinius Secundus (or Secundinus).

Domaszewski knew that the first man had been a *tribunus laticlavius* at Lambaesis, from his dedication to the *genius tribunicialis* ("guardian spirit of the tribunes") there, giving his full name as Quintus Flavius Balbus.[23] As it turns out, his senatorial career would eventually take him on to the praetorian governorship of Arabia, as attested by a series of statue-bases from the legionary fortress at Bostra, followed by the consulship in a so far unknown year.[24] The second man Domaszewski identified as the same Tiberius Teltonius Marcellus who

---

[21] A. von Domaszewski, *Die Rangordnung des römischen Heeres* (Bonn 1908), p. 130, citing *CIL* VIII, 18078.

[22] See also *infra*, p. 44, for this process of *damnatio memoriae*, inflicted upon emperors who were deemed to be unworthy of commemoration.

[23] *AE* 1898, 12.

[24] Arabia: *CIL* III, 95. Consul: *CIL* XIV, 2576.

set up a dedication to Saturnus Frugifer ("fruit-bearing Saturn") while *praefectus castrorum* of the Third Augusta Legion.[25] From these clues, Domaszewski suggested that this was a list of the legion's *trib[uni et praefectus]* ("tribunes and prefect"), and that the remaining names (only one of which survived) must have belonged to the legion's equestrian tribunes.

It is an elegant solution, given that, having named the *tribunus laticlavius* and the *praefectus castrorum*, the only remaining officers are the *tribuni angusticlavii* (or "narrow-striped tribunes" in reference to the purple stripe worn by equestrians), several of whom appear to have served simultaneously in each legion. We may, however, wonder whether the order of names better reflects the social status of the individuals, rather than the strict hierarchy of command. Of course, as Domaszewski well knew, in the unavoidable absence of the *legatus legionis*, only another senator could deputize, and there are a handful of known cases where the *tribunus laticlavius* acted *pro legato* ("in place of the legate") until a new commander could be appointed.[26] Nevertheless, it would seem more sensible to entrust the temporary command of a legion to the *praefectus castrorum*, as the most experienced individual, and this is indeed what we find in AD 60, when the

---

[25] *CIL* VIII, 2666 = *ILS* 4449. Marcellus' tombstone, discovered recently near Tivoli (Italy), confirms that this post was the culmination of his career: *AE* 2011, 204.

[26] Domaszewski, *op. cit.* (n. 21), p. 172 n. 2, citing Tac., *Hist.* 3.9 and four inscriptions (*CIL* X, 4749; XI, 1834 = *ILS* 1000; XIII, 6763 = *ILS* 1188; *ILS* 8834).

Second Augusta Legion was evidently under the command of its prefect, Poenius Postumus.[27] After all, Tacitus implies that it was usual for young men to squander the opportunity of their tribunate indulging themselves in "pleasure-seeking and going on leave",[28] suggesting that, under normal circumstances, the *tribunus laticlavius* served only as a senatorial cipher.

Domaszewski's second theory is more easily dismissed, as, besides the two men cited by him,[29] no other *tribuni laticlavii* have ever come to light in command of so-called vexillations. On the contrary, this seems usually to have been a task entrusted to an equestrian tribune,[30] who, as we have seen, would have been of more mature years with more military experience, or to a legionary centurion;[31] or, indeed, to a

---

[27] Tac., *Ann.* 14.37.

[28] Tac., *Agr.* 5.1.

[29] A. von Domaszewski, *op. cit.* (n. 21), p. 172 n. 3, citing L. Roscius Aelianus (*CIL* XIV, 3612 = *ILS* 1025; see *infra*, p. 43) and the early senator Torquatus Novellius Atticus (*CIL* XIV, 3602 = *ILS* 950).

[30] *E.g.*, Gaius Valerius Rufus, equestrian tribune of the Seventh Claudia Legion, "sent by the emperor Nerva Trajan ... with a detachment on the Cyprus campaign" (*AE* 1912, 179 = *ILS* 9491: *missus cum vexillo ab Imp(eratore) Nerva Traiano ... Cyprum in expeditionem*); or Sextus Attius Senecio, equestrian tribune of the Tenth Gemina Legion, "sent by the deified Hadrian to [lead] a detachment on the Jewish campaign (*CIL* VI, 3505: *missus a divo Hadriano in expeditione Iudaica ad vexilla[tionem deducendam]*).

[31] *E.g.*, the *centurio princeps* (centurion ranked in second place beneath the chief centurion) Antonius Valentinus, in charge of a detachment of the Fourth Scythica Legion and the Sixteenth Flavia Firma Legion (*AE* 1940, 220: *pr(aepositus) ve[x(illationum) leg(ionum)*

combination of the two, such as the detachment of the Fifteenth Apollinaris Legion in Armenia, commanded by Aurelius Labrese, one of the legion's centurions, and the tribune Licinius Saturninus.[32] Perhaps unsurprisingly, the *praefectus castrorum* seems rarely if ever to have fulfilled this role,[33] as he was required to look after the fortress, but having laid down his prefecture, he was free to take up a special command as *praepositus vexillationum* ("commander of detachments").[34]

Fortunately, the body of inscriptions upon which such studies rest continues to grow, year by year, and with it the possibility, not only of learning more about the Roman army, but also of gradually coming closer to resolving such conundrums as the fate of the Ninth Legion.

III]I Scyt(hicae) et XVI F(laviae) F(irmae) P(iae) F(idelis)); Marcus Ennius Illadianus, centurion of the Fifth Macedonica Legion, in charge of a detachment of the legion "and its auxiliaries" (*AE* 1990, 868: *vexil(lationem) l[eg(ionis) V Mac(edonicae)] et auxili(i)s eius*).

[32] *CIL* III, 6052 = *ILS* 394; *cf. AE* 1910, 161 = *ILS* 9117, for a similar arrangement.

[33] Tacitus records an early instance of a *praefectus castrorum* in charge of an outpost of *vexillarii*, but no later examples are known: Tac., *Ann.* 1.38.

[34] The phrase is found on the fragmentary dedication of an ex-*praefectus castrorum* (*CIL* VI, 31871: *praeposit(us) v[exillat(ionum) per --] et Raet(iam) et Noric(um)*); cf. Gaius Velius Rufus, who moved from the post of *primus pilus* to serve as "prefect of detachments from nine legions" (*ILS* 9200: *praef(ectus) vexillariorum leg(ionum) VIIII*, followed by a list of eight legions).

Figure 1: Tombstone of Rufinus from York

1 A VERY INTERESTING STONE

O N 7 OCTOBER 1854, with the Crimean War dominating the news, readers of *The York Herald and General Advertiser* might easily have missed the report, tucked away at the bottom of an inside page, announcing the discovery of "a very interesting Roman stone" in the city of York.

York, of course, was the site of the Roman legionary fortress of Eburacum. In the mid-nineteenth century, it was suspected that the Ninth Legion had once been based here. Indeed, visitors to the Yorkshire Museum could stand face to face with one of this legion's junior officers, Lucius Duccius Rufinus, *signif(er) leg(ionis) VIIII* ("standard-bearer of the Ninth Legion"), for his likeness is depicted on a tombstone (fig. 1), rescued some years earlier "from the brutish workman who had broke it in the middle" when it was extracted during construction work in Micklegate, behind York's Holy Trinity Church.[35]

Throughout the 1840s and 1850s, the Revd Charles Wellbeloved, a local antiquarian who, in his retirement, assumed the role of Curator of the Antiquities in the Yorkshire Museum, had popularized Roman York in his various publications.[36] So the discovery of a Roman artefact would not have been entirely unexpected in 1854. However, the substantial inscribed slab (fig. 2), measuring some three feet by three feet, unearthed by workmen digging a drain in King's Square, near the site of the Roman fortress's south-east gate, proved to be of more than local interest.

Although Wellbeloved was in his 80s by now, and suffering from poor health, the onus fell upon him as the local expert to elucidate the discovery for the benefit of the public. The slab carried six lines of Latin text, and although the left and right edges had been broken off prior to its discovery, Wellbeloved was confident that the message on the slab could be restored. In fact, his initial assessment for *The York Herald* was broadly correct, though he was constrained by a belief that "the slab is so nearly perfect that the few letters which are

---

[35] The stone (*CIL* VII, 243 = *RIB* 673) was already known to Fabretti, *op. cit.* (n. 3), p. 340 (no. 515), whence it was picked up by Orelli, *op. cit.* (n. 4), Vol. 1, p. 472 (no. 2704), but not by Dessau.

[36] C. Wellbeloved, *Eburacum, or York under the Romans* (London 1842). He also authored *A Descriptive Account of the Antiquities in the Grounds and in the Museum of the Yorkshire Philosophical Society* (York 1852; 2nd edn. 1854; 3rd edn. 1858).

wanting to complete the inscription may be readily and confidently supplied".

Figure 2: The "very interesting Roman stone" from York

This degree of confidence was a little optimistic, and his proposed restoration was clearly hampered by his belief that only a few letters were lacking on either side of the fragment, although Orelli's compendium (a copy of which he evidently had to hand) amply demonstrated the standard layout of a Roman imperial inscription and the abbreviations likely to be encountered there.

Wellbeloved recognized that the slab carried the name of the emperor Trajan, who reigned from AD 98 until AD 117, but deciphering a Roman inscription is a little like solving a word puzzle. And in order to make sense of the process, some knowledge of imperial nomenclature is required.

In common with previous emperors, Trajan accumulated the various titles and honours that proved his imperial legitimacy and ensured his sovereignty. Any official inscription was sure to quote these titles *in extenso*.

For example, all emperors, since the days of the imperial founder Augustus, had taken the sacred titles of "high priest" (*pontifex maximus*) and "father of his country" (*pater patriae*). The fact that Wellbeloved could find no space for the latter title in his restoration should have caused him pause for thought. Equally, the absence of any reference to Trajan's consulship makes Wellbeloved's restoration highly unusual, as a glance through Orelli's compendium would have confirmed.[37] The consulship (abbreviated to *COS* on inscriptions)

---

[37] Orelli, *op. cit.* (n. 4), Vol. 1, pp. 188-193 for inscriptions of Trajan, numbered 782-804. Most interesting is no. 787 (= *CIL* XII, 105 =

was the highest magistracy open to Roman senators; two consuls opened each year, which was henceforth known by their names, and generally stood down after an interval of a few months to make way for so-called *suffecti* ("substitutes"), thus increasing the pool of men who were qualified to fill a consular role. An iterated consulship was a great honour, and very few men achieved a third, except for the emperors, who frequently took several. (Trajan, in fact, filled the office six times.)

As far as the other names and titles are concerned, by the mid-first century, it had become usual to begin the emperor's name with *Imperator Caesar* and to append the name *Augustus*, while Trajan, in particular, had thought it expedient to underline his legal adoption by his predecessor, especially as that predecessor had subsequently been deified. Thus, he not only took the name "Nerva" from his adoptive father, as was his right, but he emphasized the fact that he was *divi Nervae filius* ("son of the divine Nerva").

Wellbeloved, to his credit, noticed the traces of another of Trajan's titles: namely, *imperator* in the sense of "conquering general", for it had become traditional for an emperor to take such an imperatorial acclamation upon his elevation, and to follow it with a numeral, which was incremented with each major victory won by his armies. So, in AD 101, for example, following a Roman victory in Dacia (present-day Romania), Trajan became *imperator II*, or "acclaimed as conquering

---

ILS 289), showing the normal sequence of Trajan's nomenclature during the period 10 December AD 107 to 9 December AD 108.

general twice",[38] while in subsequent years, he received additional acclamations until he reached a total of thirteen.

Finally, it became increasingly common for any emperor who had conquered a particular people to emphasize the fact by adopting a suitable title. Trajan, for example, added the titles *Germanicus* ("Conqueror of the Germans") and *Dacicus* ("Conqueror of the Dacians") to his already lengthy nomenclature, followed latterly (and over-optimistically, as it turned out) by *Parthicus* ("Conqueror of the Parthians") in the year before his death. Here again, Wellbeloved should have been wary, as his initial restoration left room only for *Germanicus*. However, a month later, when he came to address the Yorkshire Philosophical Society, he had settled upon a version that correctly included *Dacicus* as well.[39]

The importance of the stone lay in the fact that it could be precisely dated, for the sequence of imperial titles occupying the first five lines, particularly Trajan's twelfth year of tribunician power, narrowed it down to the twelve-month period ending on 9 December AD 108.

Wellbeloved was troubled by the absence of a verb to explain what was done *per legionem VIIII Hispanicam* ("by the

---

[38] Orelli, *op. cit.* (n. 4), Vol. 1, p. 188, no. 783, a milestone from the Puteoli-Naples road, begun by Nerva and completed by Trajan in AD 102, demonstrates this title; *cf. CIL* X, 6928 = *ILS* 285.

[39] C. Wellbeloved, "Observations on a Roman inscription lately discovered in York: read at the monthly meeting of the Yorkshire Philosophical Society, Nov. 7, 1854", *Proceedings of the Yorkshire Philosophical Society. A selection* (London 1855), pp. 282-286.

Ninth Hispanic Legion").[40] His first thought was to insert *instruxit* ("prepared") at the end of line 5,[41] but he finally settled upon the phrase *F(aciendum) C(uravit)* ("arranged for (this) to be done") as being "commonly used in similar inscriptions". However, this phrase is usually encountered only on tombstones, whereas the verb most commonly found in military building inscriptions is simply *fecit* ("built (this)").

In fact, as the German scholar Emil Hübner saw when he came to publish the inscription in *CIL* VII, the end of the fifth line probably originally read *CO(n)S(ul) V P(ater) P(atriae)* ("consul for the fifth time, father of his country"), to match other imperial inscriptions erected in this year.[42]

Hübner did not venture to suggest what building work might have occasioned the creation of the slab. Nor, indeed, did Wellbeloved, and his son-in-law and successor as Curator in the 1860s, the Revd John Kenrick, suggested only that "it must have been intended to have been affixed to some building, and a building of considerable magnitude and solidity";

---

[40] See *infra*, p. 37 on the legion's correct title.

[41] This verb seldom occurs on military inscriptions, so it seems likely that Wellbeloved must have known *CIL* VII, 445 = *RIB* 1091, a rare instance in connection with the construction of a baths-basilica beside the fort at Lanchester, published by C. Hunter, "A letter from Mr Christopher Hunter to Dr Martin Lister concerning some Roman inscriptions found near Durham", *Philosophical Transactions* Vol. 22, no. 266 (1700), pp. 656-658.

[42] E. Hübner, *Corpus Inscriptionum Latinarum* Vol. 7: *Inscriptiones Britanniae Latinae* (Berlin 1873), p. 64, no. 241, where he mistakenly dated it to AD 108/9. For another inscription of AD 108, see *supra*, n. 37.

but it is evident that, in his opinion, the "work worthy of commemoration on a tablet so large and beautiful" might have been the construction of the fortress walls themselves.[43] Hübner concurred.[44]

Unfortunately, Wellbeloved and Kenrick's ignorance of Continental scholarship concealed from them the wider significance of the stone for legionary studies.[45] As far as they were concerned, its sole importance lay in the fact that "this is one of the most ancient of Roman inscriptions in Britain".[46]

---

[43] J. Kenrick, *A Selection of Papers on Subjects of Archaeology and History* (London 1864), pp. 182-197.

[44] E. Hübner, *op. cit.* (n. 42), p. 61, stating that *Traianus a. 108 opus aliquod, turrim puto murive partem, extrui fecit* ("Trajan, in the year 108, caused some work to be constructed, a tower, I believe, or part of the wall").

[45] In fact, it was an anonymous correspondent to the *York Herald* who pointed out that "it is a valuable discovery, inasmuch as it fixes a precise period when the ninth legion was in York".

[46] This original statement in Wellbeloved's *Descriptive Account* (n. 36, p. 32) was repeated in successive editions. When Kenrick's successor as Curator, James Raine, reissued it as *A Hand-Book to the Antiquities in the Grounds and Museum of the Yorkshire Philosophical Society by the late Rev. Charles Wellbeloved* (York 1881), he added the fantastic suggestion that "it is quite possible that it recorded the erection of the Imperial Palace" (p. 43).

2 A PHANTOM TILE

In Wellbeloved's day, one of the classic texts on Roman Britain was *Britannia Romana*, written by the Northumberland antiquarian Revd. John Horsley over a century before. As late as 1933, it was still recommended as "the great storehouse of information on the Roman antiquities of Britain".[47]

Horsley would have welcomed the York inscription with open arms. He lamented the fact that, between the departure of Agricola (following the famous battle of Mons Graupius in AD 83) and the arrival of Hadrian in AD 122, the history of Britain was hidden in shadows: "the more so, because we cannot borrow any light or assistance from any Roman inscriptions in Britain, there being none now extant, which we can be certain are so ancient as this".[48]

---

[47] J. Horsley, *Britannia Romana, or the Roman Antiquities of Britain* (London 1732). The quote is from R.G. Collingwood (ed.), *The Handbook to the Roman Wall* (9th edn. Newcastle-upon-Tyne 1933), p. 2, repeating the words of the Revd J. Collingwood Bruce, *The Wallet-book of the Roman Wall* (London 1863), p. 2.

[48] Horsley, *op. cit.* (n. 47), p. 49.

Nevertheless, by diligent study, Horsley had identified the various legions of the Roman army in Britain. Although largely ignorant of the brief presence of the Second Adiutrix (the legion left few inscriptions, only one of which was known to Horsley), he deduced from the pages of the historian Tacitus that four legions had formed the original garrison of the province under the emperors Claudius and Nero, and he knew that, of those four, the Fourteenth Gemina had departed in AD 70.[49] He also knew that the Second Augusta and the Twentieth Valeria Victrix had remained in the island for the duration of the Roman occupation.[50] That left only the Ninth Legion.

However, as a native of Hadrian's Wall country, Horsley could not ignore the abundant evidence for the presence of the Sixth Victrix Legion in the province. And as a well-read scholar, he was well aware that an inscribed statue base, noticed by sixteenth-century antiquarians prior to its disappearance from Trajan's forum in Rome, carried important information about this legion's movements.

The missing inscription (fig. 3) detailed the career of Marcus Pontius Laelianus, who had served as tribune of the Sixth Victrix Legion, *cum qua ex Germ(ania) in Brittan(iam) transiit* ("with which he crossed over from Germany to Britain").[51]

---

[49] As reported by Tac., *Hist.* 4.68.

[50] Cassius Dio, *Roman History* 55.23.2 and 23.6, has them in Britain during his lifetime c. AD 210.

[51] Broken into two parts, the top section was published as *CIL* VI, 1497 (*ILS* 1094), while the bottom section was published as *CIL* VI, 1549 (*ILS* 1100), in the belief that the texts did not belong together.

Figure 3: Boissard's version of Laelianus' statue base

His employment only a few years thereafter as *trib(unus) pleb(is) candidatus Imp(eratoris) divi Hadriani* ("tribune of the

---

The version combining the two texts, suggested by Jean-Jacques Boissard and published by Gruter, *op. cit.* (n. 2), p. 457 no. 2 (whence Orelli no. 3186), is now usually accepted, though in the nineteenth century, the tribune of the Sixth Victrix was considered to be a different (unnamed) person: cf. Wilmanns, *op. cit.* (n. 6), Vol. 1, p. 184, no. 637.

plebs as candidate of the emperor, the divine Hadrian") placed his military tribunate, and thus the arrival of the Sixth Victrix Legion in Britain, squarely in the reign of Hadrian.[52]

As for the Ninth Legion, Horsley could find no trace of it, though he was willing to accept, on the basis of the tombstone of Rufinus (fig. 1), that it had been based at York. Last mentioned in AD 82 by the historian Tacitus (in *Agricola* 26.1), its ultimate fate perplexed the Northumberland antiquarian: "it might possibly be broke", he wrote (meaning that the legion could have been destroyed), "or incorporated with the *legio sexta victrix*".[53]

This last suggestion was prompted by the alleged discovery, shortly before 1707, of a stamped tile bearing the inscription LEG IX VIC, instead of the expected LEG IX HISP.[54] Though Horsley never saw the tile (and nor did anyone else besides the owner), he was happy to fabricate a sketch of it in his "Collection of Roman Inscriptions & Sculptures found in Britain".[55]

---

[52] Horsley had no knowledge of the inscription linking the Sixth Victrix Legion in Britain with the Hadrianic governor Aulus Platorius Nepos (*RIB* 1427), which was only discovered in 1936.

[53] Horsley, *op. cit.* (n. 47), p. 80.

[54] R. Thoresby, "A letter ... concerning some Roman inscriptions found at York, proving that the Ninth Legion some time resided there", *Philosophical Transactions* Vol. 25, no. 305 (1707), pp. 2194-2196, reprinted in his *Ducatus Leodiensis, or the Topography of the ancient and populous town and parish of Leedes* (London 1715), p. 562

[55] Horsley, *op. cit.* (n. 47), p. 192, no. 63 (Yorkshire), fig. IX.

Of course, eighteenth-century antiquarians had little idea of the significance of Roman brick and tile. For example, reporting on a "curious brick" discovered at Chester, with LEG XX VV stamped near the centre, Horsley commented on the "ledge turn'd up on each side about an inch broad, and raised an inch above the inner surface of the brick",[56] without apparently realizing that he was describing a *tegula*, the classic Roman roof-tile (*cf.* fig. 4).

Whenever the legions built in stone, they roofed in tile. This necessitated the establishment of a tilery in the vicinity of their fortress, manned by the specialist *scandularii* ("roof-tile makers") who were amongst the diverse artisans found in every legion. The building process required tiles of various shapes and sizes: roofs were clad with alternating rows of *tegulae* (the flat tiles with characteristic edge flanges) and *imbrices* (semi-cylindrical tiles positioned to cover the junction between these flanges); heated rooms had their floors raised on piles of flat, square *pedales* and their walls lined with hollow rectangular *tubuli* to allow hot air to circulate from a furnace; and flat brick-like tiles were used to line ovens and sewers or to lay bonding courses in stone wall construction.

For reasons that have never become fully apparent, the practice soon arose of stamping tiles with the name of the

---

[56] Horsley, *op. cit.* (n. 47), p. 318, illustrated on p. 192, no. 67 (Cheshire), fig. VII. Hübner reported the tile-stamp as *CIL* VII, 1225c. It appears to be of the type recorded as *RIB* 2463.4, which W. Thompson Watkin, *Roman Cheshire* (Liverpool, 1886), p. 119, characterized as "the ordinary red tiles of the legion which have been found at Chester in immense numbers".

legion responsible for their manufacture. In Britain, this practice seems to have been adopted only in the later first century, for none of the tiles discovered at the Neronian fortress at Exeter were stamped. Thus, it was probably the Trajanic refurbishment of the York fortress that led the Ninth Legion to initiate the stamping of tiles there. But this chain of events was entirely unknown to the antiquarians of the eighteenth and early nineteenth centuries.

They were likewise ignorant of the tilery used by the Ninth Legion at York, which was only discovered in 1970, some distance to the east of the fortress at Peaseholm Green.[57] Few of the legion's stamped tiles were known to the early antiquarians, and those few were stray finds unearthed by workmen, with the single exception of the following peculiar discovery.

In 1768, the first of several so-called "tile tombs" was unearthed, consisting of a cremation burial with grave goods protected by a covering of roof-tiles, in this case six *tegulae* and three *imbrices*, "built up in the form of the roof of a house, making a triangle with the ground below".[58] Another two

---

[57] E. King, "Roman kiln material from the Borthwick Institute, Peaseholm Green: a report for York Excavation Group", *The Antiquaries Journal* Vol. 54 (1974), pp. 213-217.

[58] J. Burton, "An account of a Roman sepulchre, found near York, in 1768", *Archaeologia* Vol. 2 (1773), pp. 177-180. The quotation is from W. Hargrove, *History and Description of the Ancient City of York*, Vol. 1 (York 1818), p. 239. Another similar tomb was discovered in 1840: Raine, *op. cit.* (n. 46), p. 61.

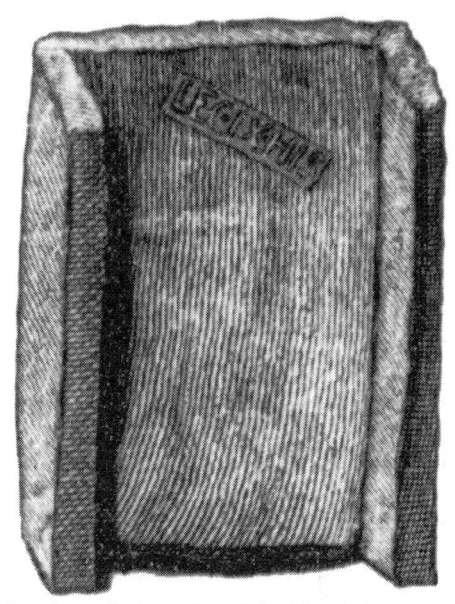

Figure 4: Roofing tile (tegula) of the Ninth Legion

tegulae, used to block the open ends of the structure, were each stamped LEG IX HIS (fig. 4).[59]

Throughout the nineteenth century, similar stamped tiles of the Ninth Legion continued to accrue, until in 1858, the Yorkshire Museum had so many that "at the request of the British Museum, specimens of tiles, with the stamp of the 8th and 9th legion, have been furnished to the national collection of Roman Antiquities".[60] Meanwhile, the existence of the single LEG IX VIC tile became an article of faith, repeated down

---

[59] Hübner reported this tile-stamp as *CIL* VII, 1224a. It is of the type recorded as *RIB* 2462.5.

[60] *Annual Report of the Council of the Yorkshire Philosophical Society for MDCCCLVIII* (York 1859), p. 13. The reference to "the 8th" legion is probably a typographic error for the Sixth Victrix Legion.

to the time of Wellbeloved.[61] Even Hübner included the inscription, though he thought it suspicious.[62]

Nevertheless, Horsley was encouraged in his belief by a passage in Dio's *Roman History*,[63] describing how "some [of Augustus' legions] were disbanded altogether, others were amalgamated with other legions by Augustus himself and by later emperors"; but he omitted the final part of the sentence, where Dio explains that "this is how such legions have come to bear the name Twin".

Unfortunately, there was no record of the Ninth Legion having been twinned in this way,[64] or of a legion having been "broke", as happened, for example, in AD 161, when the Parthians, "completely surrounding an entire Roman legion stationed under Severianus at Elegeia, a place in Armenia, shot it down and annihilated it with its officers".[65]

Horsley's theory coloured the opinions of all who came after. When, for example, the Yorkshire surgeon and antiquarian Francis Drake came to write about the Ninth Legion in his history of York, he claimed that it was "probable that it had been broke, perhaps by Severus, and the soldiers that

---

[61] Thoresby's report found its way into Bishop Edmund Gibson's widely-read edition of Camden's iconic *Britannia* (London 1722), Vol. 2, p. 878. Wellbeloved, *op. cit.* (n. 36, 1842), p. 35.

[62] *CIL* VII, 1224e, nowadays regarded as a false reading; see *RIB* 2462.17.

[63] Dio, *Roman History* 55.23.7.

[64] Dio implies that this was the origin of the legions named *Gemina* ("Twin").

[65] Dio, *Roman History* 71.2.1

composed it thrown into the sixth".[66] The same tale of the legion "early broken and incorporated with the Sixth" was repeated by subsequent commentators throughout the eighteenth and nineteenth centuries.[67]

---

[66] F. Drake, *Eboracum, or the History and Antiquities of the City of York* (York 1736), p. 50. Why he selected the emperor Septimius Severus (r. AD 193-211) is not stated.

[67] *E.g.* Hargrove, *op. cit.* (n. 58), p. 34; Wellbeloved, *op. cit.* (n. 36, 1842), p. 35. It was still repeated by Raine, *op. cit.* (n. 46), p. 127, though with less conviction.

3 ONE OF OUR LEGIONS IS MISSING

BY CHANCE, in the same year that saw the discovery of the slab at York, the young German scholar Wilhelm Pfitzner published "A general history of the imperial legions to the time of Hadrian".[68] Having traced the movements of the legions throughout the first century AD, he pronounced that changes in their number and distribution under Trajan and Hadrian could be discerned from "two almost identical legionary inscriptions that are preserved on two rounded marble pillars at Rome".[69]

Pfitzner's timing was perfect. Only a few years earlier, the Hannover scholar Karl Ludwig Grotefend had placed the study of the imperial legions on a firm foundation with the publication of a lengthy article in August Pauly's multi-

---

[68] W.H. Pfitzner, "Allgemeine Geschichte der römischen Kaiserlegionen bis Hadrian", *Der Schulschriften des großherzoglichen Friedrich-Franz-Gymnasiums* Vol. 4 (1854), pp. 1-25.

[69] Pfitzner, *op. cit.* (n. 68), p. 24, citing Orelli nos. 3368 and 3369.

volume encyclopedia of classical antiquity.[70] Grotefend was something of an expert on Roman legions; the son of the philologist Georg Friedrich Grotefend, who was celebrated for having cracked the enigma of cuneiform script, young Karl Ludwig had even chosen the legions as the subject of his school leaving essay for entry into university in 1825.[71]

Grotefend it was who first realized that the abbreviation *HISP* found on many of the legion's inscriptions should be expanded to read "Hispana". Until then, scholars had been unable to agree upon the correct title for the Ninth Legion. Pfitzner avoided the debate by referring to the legion only by its numeral,[72] while the Revd Wellbeloved thought that it was named *Hispanica*, though he never explained why. Grotefend initially used the title *Hispaniensis*, but later preferred *Hispana*, on the basis of a tombstone found in Rome.[73] Ironically, the legion does appear originally to have been named *Hispaniensis* ("from Spain"), no doubt as a result of service there during the emperor Augustus' final conquest of the Cantabrians

---

[70] C.L. Grotefend, "Legio (Geschichte)", in *Real-Encyclopädie der classischen Alterthumswissenschaft* Vol. 4 (Stuttgart 1846), pp. 868-901.

[71] It was more probably his later article, "Kurze Uebersicht der Geschichte der römischen Legionen von Cäsar bis Gallienus", *Zeitschrift für die Alterthumswissenschaft* 1840, Nos. 79-81, col. 641-668, that recommended him as a contributor to Pauly's *Real-Encyclopädie*.

[72] In this, he simply followed Tacitus, who similarly never mentions the legion's title; cf. *Agr.* 26; *Ann.* 4.23; 14.32, 38; *Hist.* 3.22.

[73] *CIL* VI, 3639, known to Grotefend from Fabretti, *op. cit.* (n. 3), p. 705, no. 253.

during the years 26 BC until 19 BC.[74] This form of the legion's title was first noticed on an inscription from Valenza in the north of Italy, but this would have been unknown to Grotefend.[75]

He was also well aware of the memorial set up at Rome by Gaius Julius Erucianus Crispus "to his excellent friend" Lucius Aemilius Karus, listing the career of this highly successful senator in great detail, including the fact that he had served as *trib(unus) militum leg(ionis) VIIII Hispanae* ("military tribune of the Ninth Hispana Legion"), thus finally confirming the usual form of the legion's title.[76]

Grotefend's entry in Pauly's *Real-Encyclopädie* briefly encapsulated the history of each legion, as it was then understood. The Ninth Legion, he knew, had lain, from the days of Augustus, in Pannonia,[77] the province occupying parts of present-day Austria, Hungary, Slovenia, and Croatia, which was

---

[74] For an account of this war, see Dio, *Roman History* 53.25.2-8, 29.1-2; 54.5.1-3, 11.2-5; Florus, *Epitome of All the Wars* 2.33.

[75] *CIL* V, 7443 = *AE* 1987, 414. The legion also has this name on *AE* 1975, 446, an early tombstone discovered in the 1950s at Cremona, and appears as *Leg(io) VIIII Hispanie(n)s(is)* on *ILS* 2321, a tombstone discovered in 1886 at Cales in Campania. All three are thought to date from the reign of Augustus, when people would still have remembered that the legion had been withdrawn "from Spain".

[76] *CIL* VI, 1333 = *ILS* 1077, known to Grotefend from C. Kellermann, *Vigilum Romanorum latercula duo coelimontana* (Rome 1835), p. 67, no. 243, whence Henzen added it to Orelli, *op. cit.* (n. 4), Vol. 3, p. 202, no. 6049. The inscription was already in Gruter, *op. cit.* (n. 2), p. 1025, no. 2.

[77] Tac., *Ann.* 1.23 and 30, mentions the legion there in AD 14.

then under the governorship of Quintus Junius Blaesus. In AD 20, it was sent with Blaesus to reinforce the army of north Africa against constant raiding by the Musulamians under their leader Tacfarinas. Tacitus records how a traveller on the Flaminian Way "overtook a legion that was being marched from Pannonia to the city of Rome, and thereafter for the protection of Africa".[78] By AD 24, Blaesus had acquired *ornamenta triumphalia* ("triumphal ornaments", though he had not earned them, as Tacfarinas remained at large), and the legion returned to Pannonia. Here Grotefend missed the opportunity to cite the laudatory inscription set up, "by decree of the decurions" in the town of Brixia, to the grandly named Publius Cornelius Lentulus Scipio, *legatus Ti(berii) Caesaris Aug(usti) leg(ionis) VIIII Hispan(ae)* ("Tiberius Caesar Augustus' legate of the Ninth Hispana Legion"), no doubt for successes in Africa.[79]

Over the next fifteen years, governors of Pannonia came and went, until the arrival of Aulus Plautius early in the reign of Claudius.[80] When he was ordered to lead the invasion of Britain in AD 43, it is likely that he took the Ninth Legion with

---

[78] Tac., *Ann.* 3.9.

[79] *CIL* V, 4329 = *ILS* 940, already noted by Orelli, *op. cit.* (n. 4), Vol. 1, p. 392, no. 2275. Scipio is mentioned in the fighting by Tacitus, *Ann.* 3.74. Blaesus' ornaments: Tac., *Ann.* 3.72. Legion returns: Tac., *Ann.* 4.23.

[80] His governorship of Pannonia was deduced from *CIL* V, 698 = *ILS* 5889 by E. Ritterling, "Die Statthalter der pannonischen Provinzen", *Archäologisch-epigraphische Mitteilungen aus Österreich-Ungarn* Vol. 20 (1898), pp. 1-40, at pp. 8-9.

him.[81] It certainly formed part of the early garrison of the province. Tacitus next mentions the legion in connection with the Boudiccan revolt of AD 60, during the governorship of Gaius Suetonius Paullinus. Taking advantage of the governor's preoccupation with the conquest of Anglesey, the tribe of the Iceni in present-day East Anglia sacked the Roman town of Colchester. In the chaos, writes Tacitus, "the victorious Britons met Petillius Cerialis, the Ninth Legion's legate, who was coming to the rescue; they routed his legion and slaughtered his infantry; Cerialis and the cavalry escaped to their *castra*, where they were defended by the fortifications".[82] In the aftermath, Tacitus reports that 2,000 legionaries were sent over from Germany, "whose arrival allowed the gaps in the Ninth to be filled with regular legionaries".[83] The *castra* ("camp") to which Cerialis had retreated was the legion's permanent fortress, nowadays reckoned to be at Lincoln, but evidence was lacking in Grotefend's day. The first tombstone from the town to name a soldier of the Ninth Legion (fig. 5) only came to light in 1840.[84]

---

[81] *CIL* V, 7165, a fragment of a memorial preserved at Turin, listing the career of an unknown senator who evidently accompanied the emperor Claudius during the invasion, may conceal a reference to this legion: cf. *AE* 2003, 776.

[82] Tac., *Ann.* 14.32.

[83] Tac., *Ann.* 14.38.

[84] The tombstone (*CIL* VII, 184 = *RIB* 256) was not commonly known until 1856, when Henzen included it in his supplement to Orelli, *op. cit.* (n. 4), Vol. 3, p. 337, no. 6676 (but unaccountably omitted it from his otherwise exemplary index). The site of the *castra* was only confirmed by archaeology in the 1940s: G. Webster, "The

Figure 5: Tombstone of Flavinus from Lincoln.

In the civil wars that followed Nero's death in AD 68, the pretender Aulus Vitellius, who survived as emperor for only eight months, bolstered his army with an 8,000-strong battle-group drawn from the legions of Britain. Men of the Ninth Legion were amongst the vast and straggling column of 60,000 unruly soldiers who followed Vitellius to Rome in July

---

legionary fortress at Lincoln", *Journal of Roman Studies* Vol. 39 (1949), pp. 57-78.

AD 69 and toiled north again to disastrous defeat at Cremona in October.[85] Marcus Valerius Saturninus, the 38-year-old *mil(es) leg(ionis) VIIII Hispanae* ("soldier of the Ninth Hispana Legion") who was buried outside the Pincian Gate at Rome, perhaps died during this summer, and was thereby spared the final indignity suffered by his colleagues.[86]

In AD 70, the new emperor Vespasian, whose forces had been victorious at Cremona, inaugurated a new expansionist phase in Britain, and it was probably now that the Ninth Legion moved its fortress to York. This, of course, was unknown to Grotefend, being only confirmed by Hübner's interpretation of Wellbeloved's inscribed slab.[87] Grotefend was reliant on Tacitus' narrative, so he next jumped forward to the governorship of Gnaeus Julius Agricola and the years of campaigning in the north of Britain that culminated in the Battle of Mons Graupius in AD 83. Tacitus reports that, in the previous year, Agricola's sixth as governor, "the enemy massed for a night attack on the Ninth Legion, as they were particularly weak", and although the Caledonian warriors managed to

---

[85] Tac., *Hist.* 2.57. At *Hist.* 2.100, Tacitus calls them *vexillarii trium Britannicarum legionum* ("detached soldiers from the three legions in Britain"), for the Fourteenth Gemina Legion had been withdrawn in its entirety; see *supra*, n. 49. Sixty-thousand soldiers: *Hist.* 2.87. The men of the Ninth are explicitly mentioned in the Vitellian battle-line at Cremona: *Hist.* 3.22.

[86] *CIL* VI, 3639; Grotefend noted the inscription's existence (*supra*, n. 73) without drawing this conclusion.

[87] Hübner, *loc. cit.* (n. 44), though Horsley (*supra*, p. 30) had earlier suggested it.

burst into the Roman camp, when reinforcements arrived and day dawned, "the men of the Ninth regained their spirits and, now that their lives were safe, they fought for glory".[88]

Grotefend linked Tacitus' description of the legion as *maxime invalida* ("particularly weak") with the career of Lucius Roscius Aelianus, *trib(unus) mil(itum) leg(ionis) IX Hispan(ae), vexillarior(um) eiusdem in expeditione Germanica* ("military tribune of the Ninth Hispana Legion, (commander) of the detached soldiers from the same legion in the German expedition").[89] This was the emperor Domitian's war of AD 83 against the Chatti, a warlike people living in the area of present-day Hessen in Germany. The clear implication of the inscription is that the legion was *maxime invalida* precisely because a battle-group of *vexillarii* ("detached soldiers") had been sent away.

It is quite unusual for a legion's senatorial tribune, as the legate's young protégé, to absent himself in this way, for in normal circumstances, this was a task for one of the legion's equestrian tribunes, who were generally all men of more mature years.[90] Aelianus evidently acquitted himself well, as he was *donatus ab Imp(eratore) Aug(usto) militarib(us) donis corona vallari et murali vexillis argenteis II hastis puris II* ("granted military decorations by the august emperor, a rampart and a mural crown, two silver flags, and two silver spears"), though it

---

[88] Tac., *Agr.* 26.
[89] *CIL* XIV, 3612 = *ILS* 1025. Grotefend knew it from Orelli, *op. cit.* (n. 4), Vol. 2, p. 123, no. 3569.
[90] See *supra*, pp. 16-17.

is interesting to note that two other senatorial tribunes who had been obliged to take on unusual responsibility were similarly rewarded: Lucius Antistius Rusticus and the man thought to be Gaius Petillius Firmus were both granted three crowns, three flags, and three silver spears by Vespasian during their service as legionary tribune; both are thought to have temporarily filled the role of an absent legate.[91]

The tell-tale use of the non-committal phrase *ab Imperatore Augusto* ("by the august emperor") in Aelianus' inscription points to Domitian, who was not well-liked to such an extent that, after his death, the senate voted to erase him from the collective memory in a process known as *damnatio memoriae* ("condemnation of remembrance"). Consequently, his name was often chipped away from inscriptions set up during his lifetime, while those set up afterwards studiously avoided explicitly mentioning him.

Grotefend was satisfied that the Ninth Legion still existed under the emperor Trajan, a conclusion he drew (probably erroneously, as we shall see) from the memorial to Tiberius Claudius Vitalis.[92] According to the inscription, Vitalis had evidently turned his back on the *militia equestris* ("equestrian military service") of his fellow *equites* for a career in the legionary centurionate. Over the course of eleven years, he

---

[91] Rusticus: *AE* 1925, 126. Firmus: *CIL* XI, 1834 = *ILS* 1000, with *AE* 1980, 468.

[92] *CIL* VI, 3584 = *ILS* 2656. Noted by J. Mazochius, *Epigrammata Antiquae Urbis* (Rome 1521), p. 48, as being "in the church of Saint Basil", its whereabouts are currently unknown. Grotefend knew it from Orelli, *op. cit.* (n. 4), Vol. 2, pp. 103-104, no. 3454.

criss-crossed the empire, transferring from legion to legion, weighed down by military decorations. Having moved from the Fifth Macedonica to the First Italica Legion, he was *donis d(onatus) torquib(us) armill(is) phaler(is) corona va[l(ari)] bello Dacico* ("granted decorations of torcs, armlets, discs, and a rampart crown in the Dacian War"); and after a transfer to the First Minervia, he was *[it]er(um) donis d(onatus) torquib(us) armil[l(is)] phaler(is) corona val[l(ari)] bello Dacico* ("again granted decorations of torcs, armlets, discs, and a rampart crown in the Dacian War"). He then served in two of the legions of Britain, the Twentieth Valeria Victrix followed by the Ninth Hispana, before finally transferring to the Eleventh Claudia Legion, where he perished at the age of 41.

Besides demonstrating the remarkable career open to a legionary centurion, and the lavish set of military decorations traditionally bestowed on men of this rank, the inscription proved to Grotefend that the Ninth Legion still existed after the creation of the First Minervia by Domitian.[93]

This is, of course, a valid observation, but Grotefend evidently thought that Vitalis had won his two sets of decorations in Trajan's Dacian Wars of AD 101-102 and 105-106. However, men who had been honoured by this most admired of emperors were eager to emphasize the fact using wording like *don(is) don(atus) ab Imp(eratore) Traiano bell(o) Dac(ico)* ("granted decorations by the emperor Trajan in the Dacian

---

[93] Dio, *Roman History* 55.24.3, names Domitian as creator of the First Minervia Legion.

War").[94] The fact that Vitalis or his heirs chose to conceal the emperor's name again points to Domitian and the Dacian War of AD 86-88.

Grotefend had one final piece of evidence to produce, for he concluded, from a letter sent to the emperor Marcus Aurelius by his childhood tutor and confidante, Marcus Cornelius Fronto, that "the Romans had suffered a significant defeat under Hadrian in Britain, and it is more than likely that only then did the IX Hispana succumb".[95]

This all seemed to fit with the inscribed pillars that Pfitzner referred to, each comprising a list of Roman legions, arranged in three columns and eleven rows under the general heading *NOMINA LEG(ionum)* ("The names of the legions"). The list could readily be found in Orelli's compendium, where it had been copied from Gruter.[96] Gruter, in turn, had lifted it from an earlier collection compiled by Martin Smetius and brought to publication after his death by the Dutch scholar Justus Lipsius,[97] but it is not clear where Smetius got his text. All three collections insisted that two almost identical

---

[94] This example is from *CIL* II, 2424, which was known to Grotefend from Kellermann, *op. cit.* (n. 76), p. 35, no. 33, and correctly cited by him as evidence for the First Minervia's participation in Trajan's Dacian Wars.

[95] Grotefend, *op. cit.* (n. 70), 889, citing Fronto, *On the Parthian War* (quoted below, p. 55 and n. 111).

[96] Orelli, *op. cit.* (n. 4), Vol. 2, p. 83, nos. 3368-3369; Gruter, *op. cit.* (n. 2), p. 513.

[97] M. Smetius, *Inscriptionum antiquarum quae passim per Europam liber* (Leiden 1588), p. 86, no. 1.

inscriptions existed, the only difference being that, in one, the antepenultimate row had been omitted by the stone-cutter. The other, complete, example can nowadays be seen in the Galleria Lapidaria in the Vatican.

It is interesting to note that the first antiquarian to mention the list of legions, Bartolomeo Marliani in 1544, refers to only a single pillar.[98] And the sketch prepared fifty years later by Jean-Jacques Boissard, during his stay in Rome, shows only one pillar (fig. 6).[99] Grotefend seemed to hint that perhaps the first list printed by Orelli, with its missing line, was simply a defective transcript of the second, which (we may add) was an accurate representation of the inscription.[100]

Be that as it may, Grotefend realized that the legions were listed, column by column, in geographical sequence according to the province where they were based, with two glaring exceptions. Firstly, the Second Italica and Third Italica Legions, raised by the emperor Marcus Aurelius in around AD 165, were added at the end of the third column and thus

---

[98] B. Marliani, "De Legionibus Romanorum earumque Stationibus", prefixed to *Urbis Romae Topographia* (Rome 1544).

[99] J.-J. Boissard, *Antiquitatum seu inscriptionum et epitaphiorum quae in saxi et marmoribus Romanis videntur cum suis signis et imaginibus exacta descriptio*, Part III (Frankfurt 1597), p. 102. Note that, in row 3 of the pillar, Boissard misread XX VICTR as "X VI.CLA".

[100] E. Bormann & W. Henzen, *Corpus Inscriptionum Latinarum* Vol. 6: *Inscriptiones Urbis Romae Latinae*, Part 1 (Berlin 1876), p. 808, no. 3492, present a composite text, indicating where the defective copy *a* differs from the extant copy *b*. C. Huelsen, *ibid.*, Part 4.2 (Berlin 1902), p. 3396, no. 32901, claims (mistakenly) that Boissard describes version *a*.

Figure 6: Boissard's sketch of the legionary pillar

appeared out of geographical sequence; and secondly, the First, Second and Third Parthica Legions, raised by the emperor Septimius Severus in around AD 195, were added beneath the three columns in their own row. He sensibly concluded that the pillar had originally been set up before the creation of Marcus' Italica legions, which had been slotted in at the end; and since the Sixth Victrix was listed with the legions of Britain, the erection of the pillar must have occurred between AD 122 and 165.[101]

Most strikingly, "missing from the list", Grotefend noted, "are the *IX Hispaniensis*, which seems to have been dissolved by Hadrian (which is why the *VI Victrix* was sent to Britain at that time) and the *V Alauda*, whose dissolution is not mentioned at all".[102] Others were missing, too, as Pfitzner observed – the Fifteenth Primigenia, the Twenty-First Rapax, and the Twenty-Second Deiotariana – but according to the theory by which new legions were only raised to replace losses, these three had already gone by the reign of Hadrian.[103]

We now know that this theory was wrong, but Grotefend's achievement is remarkable, given the limited resources at his disposal, for with the exception of having exchanged Gruter for Orelli, he was working with the same source material as Horsley, a hundred years before. The advent of the *Corpus Inscriptionum Latinarum* would revolutionize the study of the legions for the next generation.

---

[101] Strictly speaking, Grotefend took AD 120 and AD 170 as the twin *termini*, but we are now able to refine the chronology somewhat. *Cf. supra*, pp. 28-30, for the arrival of the Sixth Victrix in Britain.

[102] Grotefend, *op. cit.* (n. 71), col. 663, written before he had settled upon *Hispana* as the correct form of the legion's title.

[103] *Ibid.*, col. 661.

4 THE MAN FROM MINTURNO

IN THE MEANTIME, others were laying the foundations of the fledgling science of prosopography, which is the study of persons and their careers from the evidence of inscriptions. In the forefront was the Italian count Bartolomeo Borghesi, an accomplished antiquarian who was forced, for political reasons, to retire to the Republic of San Marino in 1821 at the age of 40. From there, he maintained contact with the scholars of the day, in particular, throughout the 1840s and 1850s, with a young German named Theodor Mommsen.

Borghesi had lighted upon an important inscription first noted in 1790 by Sir Richard Colt Hoare, a man later known for his excavations in Wiltshire but who, in that year, was sight-seeing along the Via Appia from Rome to Benevento, retracing the route taken by Horace in 37 BC (as recounted in the poet's fifth satire). Turning aside at the town of Minturno,

Hoare recorded "three sepulchral memorials, which I had the good fortune to see soon after their disinterment".[104]

It was the first of these, the so-called career inscription of Lucius Burbuleius Ligarianus (fig. 7),[105] that Borghesi published, in a study that was hailed by later generations as a model of the prosopographic process.[106]

Although Borghesi was writing without the benefit of Henzen's useful index to Orelli, he had a vast knowledge of Latin epigraphy and knew of several similar inscriptions, including one of Quintus Pompeius Falco, the first Hadrianic governor of Britain.[107] Burbuleius' inscription had probably

---

[104] R. Colt Hoare, *Recollections Abroad, during the years 1788, 1789, 1790* (Bath 1815), pp. 309-310. The inscriptions were later published as *CIL* X, 6006, 6014, and 6018. A few of the less well-known abbreviations on the first of these were not understood by Hoare, so his transcript was not entirely accurate.

[105] *CIL* X, 6006 = *ILS* 1066. Henzen was able to include it in his supplement to Orelli, *op. cit.* (n. 4), Vol. 3, p. 296, no. 6484. Similarly, Wilmanns, *op. cit.* (n. 6), Vol. 1, p. 386, no. 1181.

[106] B. Borghesi, *Memoria sopra un'iscrizione del console L. Burbuleio Optato Ligariano serbata nel Museo Reale di Napoli* (Naples 1838), reprinted in *Oeuvres complètes de Bartolomeo Borghesi* Vol 4, *Oeuvres épigraphiques* 2 (Paris 1865), pp. 103-178. Borghesi perhaps got his copy of the text from Kellermann, who is known to have visited San Marino in the 1830s and could previously have seen the stone in Naples Museum.

[107] *CIL* X, 6321 = *ILS* 1035, first published by E.Q. Visconti, *Monumenti Gabini della Villa Pinciana* (Rome 1797; 2nd edn. Milan 1835), pp. 156-7. Henzen incorporated several improvements made by Borghesi, when he included it in his supplement to Orelli, *op. cit.* (n. 4), Vol. 3, p. 82, no. 5451. Similarly, Wilmanns, *op. cit.* (n. 6), Vol. 1, p. 380, no. 1170.

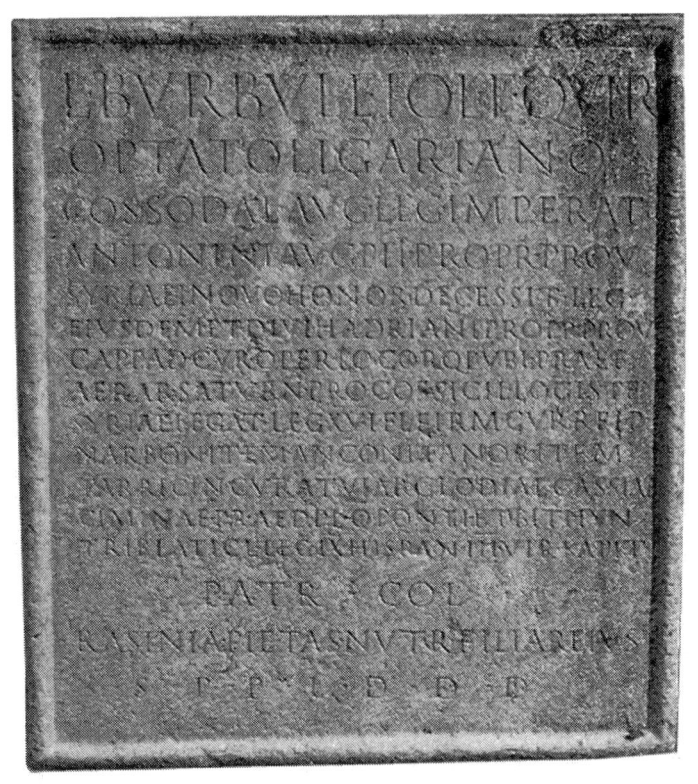

Figure 7: Career inscription of Burbuleius

once graced the plinth of a statue. The closing lines of the text indicate that *Rasinia Pietas nutr(ix) filiar(um) eius s(ua) p(ecunia) p(osuit) l(ocus) d(atus) d(ecreto) d(ecurionum)* ("Rasinia Pietas, wet-nurse of his daughters, set this up with her own money; the space was granted by decree of the decurions"). Thus, the statue had been paid for by a private individual, while the town council of Minturno had given permission for its erection in a public space. The antepenultimate line, set in slightly larger letters so as to catch the eye of the passer-by, gives us the reason for the council's decision: Burbuleius had been a *patr(onus) col(oniae)* ("patron of the colony"), no doubt in recognition of some benefaction bestowed upon the town, which was a *colonia civium Romanorum* ("colony of Roman citizens").

Like numerous other inscriptions of the same sort, this one explained Burbuleius' importance by listing the sequence of duties and functions he performed during his lifetime in the so-called *cursus honorum*. His teenaged service as *triumvir capitalis* (one of the three minor magistrates concerned with criminal jurisdiction) suggests a lack of patronage, as few men who began their career in this post went on to hold a consular command.

This verdict gains further support from the multiplicity of praetorian posts that he held, for whereas favoured senators might be appointed consul having previously held only a legionary command and the governorship of one of the emperor's provinces, Burbuleius served in no fewer than eight posts: *curator viarum Clodiae, Cassiae, Ciminae* (the official charged with the maintenance of a road network north of Rome, comprising the via Clodia, via Cassia, and via Cimina); three times *curator rei publicae* (official charged with the administration of town property and finances) attached, respectively, to Narbo, Ancona, and Terracina; *legatus* (commander) of the Sixteenth Flavia Firma Legion, stationed on the eastern frontier; *logistes* (financial auditor) of the province of Syria; *proconsul* (senatorial governor) of Sicily; and *praefectus aerarii Saturni* (official in charge of the state treasury, housed in the temple of Saturn in Rome).

Even after his consulship, it was not all plain sailing for Burbuleius, as he became *curator operum locorumque publicorum* (official charged with the management of public buildings and spaces) before receiving his first consular governorship as *legatus pro praetore provinciae Cappadociae* (governor of the imperial province of Cappadocia).

At an early stage of his career, Burbuleius had been *trib(unus) laticl(avius) leg(ionis) IX Hispan(ae)* ("senatorial tribune of the Ninth Hispana Legion"). Although Grotefend's encyclopedia article on the legions had not yet appeared, Borghesi drew together the same sources and concluded that "this is one of the lesser known legions, having been only infrequently recorded on inscriptions".[108]

Like Grotefend, he knew that Ptolemy's *Geography*, written during the reign of Antoninus Pius (AD 138-161), recorded the headquarters of three legions in Britain, and that those legions were the Second Augusta, the Twentieth Valeria Victrix, and the Sixth Victrix. And, like Grotefend, he came to the conclusion that the latter legion had replaced the Ninth Hispana during the reign of Hadrian (AD 117-138). As corroboration, he cited "the honorific inscription of an unknown individual".[109]

Borghesi was inclined to assume that the Ninth Legion had been crushed in a rebellion, albeit one barely hinted at by history, as he readily admitted. He knew that the only evidence was the claim by the author of the *Historia Augusta* that, when

---

[108] Borghesi, *op. cit.* (n. 106), p. 9 (repr., p. 110).

[109] Borghesi, *op. cit.* (n. 106), p. 14 (repr., p. 115), citing Gruter, *op. cit.* (n. 2), p. 457 no. 2 (see pp. 28-29 n. 51 and fig. 3). The unknown individual is, of course, Marcus Pontius Laelianus.

Hadrian came to power, "the nations that Trajan had subjugated were defecting, the Moors were attacking, the Sarmatians were making war, and the Britons could not be kept under Roman control",[110] a state of affairs to which Fronto obviously alluded, when he wrote to the young Marcus Aurelius: "Under the rule of your grandfather Hadrian, what a number of soldiers were slain by the Jews, what a number by the Britons".[111]

Borghesi saw that the dating of Burbuleius' career might shed some light on the history of the Ninth Legion. The best clue came not from Burbuleius' final post as *leg(atus) Imperat(oris) Antonini Aug(usti) Pii pro pr(aetore) prov(inciae) Syriae in quo honor(e) decessit* ("propraetorian legate of the emperor Antoninus Augustus Pius, of the province of Syria, in which office he died"), but from his previous service as *leg(atus) eiusdem et divi Hadriani pro pr(aetore) prov(inciae) Cappad(ociae)* ("propraetorian legate of the same emperor and of the deified Hadrian, of the province of Cappadocia"), as this post, spanning as it did the reigns of two emperors, seemed to give a firm chronological anchor.

By chance, the most celebrated governor of Cappadocia was the philosopher and writer Lucius Flavius Arrianus (known to us as Arrian), who also served there under Hadrian. For dating purposes, it was not possible for Borghesi to exploit Arrian's own mention of the death, during his time in

---

[110] *Historia Augusta, Life of Hadrian* 5.2.
[111] Fronto, *On the Parthian War* = S.A. Naber, *M. Cornelii Frontonis et M. Aurelii Imperatoris Epistulae* (Leipzig 1867) p. 218.

Cappadocia, of King Cotys II, regent of the neighbouring Cimmerian Bosphorus,[112] as the coins of that kingdom had not yet been studied in sufficient detail to elucidate the sequence of monarchs. But Borghesi astutely observed that the historian Cassius Dio recorded another event from Arrian's governorship, the threatened invasion of the Alani, prior to his mention of Hadrian dedicating the great Temple of Olympian Zeus in Athens, which was dated to AD 132.[113]

The fact that Burbuleius' governorship of Cappadocia spanned the death of Hadrian and the accession of Antoninus Pius placed him there on 10 July AD 138, while Borghesi's belief that Burbuleius had been Arrian's immediate successor was vindicated in 1871 by the discovery of a dedication made by Arrian in AD 137 while still in post.[114]

Borghesi knew that the Cappadocian command was reserved for consulars, but without knowing the year of Burbuleius' consulship, there could be no certainty about the man's age and no prospect of dating his previous posts. Borghesi was suspicious that Burbuleius had won no military decorations, which suggested that he had been too young for

---

[112] Arrian, *Periplus of the Black Sea* 17.3, now known to have occurred in AD 131/2.

[113] Dio, *Roman History* 69.15.1 and 16.1. For the dating, *CIL* III, 548 = 7281, known to Borghesi from A. Boeckh, *Corpus Inscriptionum Graecarum* Vol. 1 (Berlin 1828), p. 412, no. 331.

[114] *ILS* 8801. The inscription was published by L. Renier, "Sur une inscription grecque relative à l'historien Flavius Arrianus", *Revue Archéologique* Vol. 33 (1877), pp. 199-205, too late for Borghesi, who died in 1860.

involvement in any of Trajan's wars and that his entire career had played out under Hadrian, "in times of profound peace".[115] But beyond that he would not speculate.

Another senator whose career Borghesi believed to be relevant was Lucius Aemilius Karus.[116] He had also served as *trib(unus) militum leg(ionis) VIIII Hispanae* ("military tribune of the Ninth Hispana Legion"), probably (Borghesi felt) after Burbuleius, as he too lacked military decorations, despite having commanded Trajan's Thirtieth Ulpia Victrix Legion and having governed the province of Arabia, conquered by Trajan in AD 106.[117]

Borghesi's technique of teasing out similarities between the senatorial careers recorded on inscriptions relied upon an encyclopedic memory. In time, the *Corpus Inscriptionum Latinarum* project, by gathering all the texts together in one set of volumes, would facilitate their organization for analytical purposes. However, the first fruits of this analysis did not appear until long after Borghesi's death, with the publication of the *Prosopographia Imperii Romani,* an alphabetical listing of the careers of all known senators. Yet without further evidence, the editor of Volume 1 could only register Burbuleius' consulship as having occurred *anno incerto sub Hadriano* ("in an unknown year under Hadrian") and made no remark about his

---

[115] Borghesi, *op. cit.* (n. 106), p. 76 (repr., p. 178).
[116] See *supra,* p. 38 and n. 76.
[117] Borghesi, *op. cit.* (n. 106), p. 57 (repr., p. 159).

tribunate in the Ninth Legion.[118] His suggestion that Aemilius Karus' governorship of Cappadocia "probably fell under Antoninus Pius", while quite likely, remains to be proven.[119]

In fact, the first chronological clue to place Karus' career into context did not appear until 1909, with the final publication of a Greek inscription that once adorned the Temple of Jupiter Helios in Gerasa, a city in the province of Arabia. The dedication, to the emperor Antoninus Pius, was set up in the month of Xanthikos (April/May) AD 143 and named Aemilius Karus as governor of Arabia.[120] Confirmation came in 2004, with the publication of the first military diploma from Arabia, which listed the auxiliary units discharging time-served veterans "in Arabia under Aemilius Carus" in AD 142.[121] Like Numidia and Judaea, this was a one-legion province, where the governor simultaneously commanded the legion (in this case, the Third Cyrenaica), and the consulship normally followed directly after. However, it was not until 2014 that

---

[118] E. Klebs, *Prosopographia Imperii Romani saeculorum I, II, III*, Vol. 1 (Berlin 1897), p. 243, no. B151.

[119] *Ibid.*, p. 27, no. A219. The suggestion owes its origin to Marquard Gude's note to Gruter, *op. cit.* (n. 2), p. 1025, no. 2, in the 1707 edition of Graevius.

[120] *AE* 1909, 236. Parts of the inscription were published by J. Germer-Durand, "Nouvelle exploration épigraphique de Gérasa", *Revue Biblique* Vol. 8 (1899), pp. 5-39, at pp. 9-10 (no. 7) and p. 20 (no. 23), and the entire text by F.M. Abel, "Nouvelles inscriptions de Djérach", *Revue Biblique* Vol. 6 (1909), pp. 448-453, at pp. 448-450.

[121] *AE* 2004, 1925, based on P. Weiß & M.P. Speidel, "Das erste Militärdiplom für Arabia", *Zeitschrift für Papyrologie und Epigraphik* Vol. 150 (2004), pp. 253-264.

Karus' consulship, long known to have been shared with Quintus Egrilius Plarianus,[122] was finally dated to March AD 144.[123]

Returning to Burbuleius, an inscription published in 1983 demonstrated not only that a daughter of his had married Marcus Messius Rusticianus, a well-to-do young man from Siarum near Seville in the province of Hispania Baetica, but also that the young man's father, Marcus Aemilius Papus, had shared the consulship with Burbuleius.[124] It finally became clear, in 1999, that the pair were in office on 19 May AD 135.[125]

If Burbuleius held the consulship at the age of 40, having benefited from the *ius liberorum*, he would have been born in AD 94 or 95. This means that his legionary tribunate would have fallen late in the reign of Trajan, perhaps in AD 114 (if, like Agricola, Burbuleius was tribune at the age of 20) or AD 117 (if, like Quintus Sicinius Maximus, at the age of 23). The same calculation suggests that Karus' tribunate should have

---

[122] The two were named on *CIL* VI, 30868, published in 1902: C. Hülsen, *Corpus Inscriptionum Latinarum* Vol. 6: *Inscriptiones Urbis Romae Latinae*, Part 4, Fascicule 2 (Berlin 1902), p. 3026. But the date was unknown.

[123] *AE* 2014, 1657, based on W. Eck & A. Pangerl, "Eine Konstitution des Antoninus Pius für die Auxilien in Syrien aus dem Jahr 144", *Zeitschrift für Papyrologie und Epigraphik* Vol. 188 (2014), pp. 255-260. *Cf.* also *AE* 2015, 1904.

[124] *AE* 1983, 517, based on J. González & A. Caballos Rufino, "Die Messii Rustici. Eine senatorische Familie aus der Baetica", *Zeitschrift für Papyrologie und Epigraphik* Vol. 52 (1983), pp. 157-171.

[125] *AE* 1999, 1352 = M. Roxan & P. Holder, *Roman Military Diplomas IV* (London 2003), pp. 489-491, no. 251.

fallen nine or ten years later, at some time in the period AD 122–127.

Of course, none of this was known to Borghesi in the 1830s. But news soon reached him of a third man whose career might shed some interesting light on the history of the Ninth Legion.

5 THE FINEST TOMB IN PETRA

NO SOONER HAD Borghesi published his study of Burbuleius' career than another inscription mentioning the Ninth Legion was drawn to his attention, by the Jesuit scholar Giampietro Secchi. He, in turn, had received news of it from the self-styled Comte Jules de Bertou.

In 1838, Bertou, a celebrated explorer of the Middle East, made a journey from the Dead Sea to the Gulf of Aqaba, during which he took a detour to Petra in present-day Jordan. His visit made him one of only half-a-dozen or so westerners who had seen the ruined city since its rediscovery by the Swiss explorer Jean Louis Burckhardt in 1812.[126]

The city was especially noted for its charming location, enclosed within a pair of parallel sandstone ridges, in the sides of which various tombs and chambers had been cut,

---

[126] J. Bertou, "Voyage de l'extrémité sud de la mar Morte à la pointe nord du golfe Elanitique", *Bulletin de la Société de Géographie* Vol. 10 (1838), pp. 18-32.

appearing "from the rock as if by magic grown".[127] Travellers generally approached from the east, along a narrow, twisting gorge called the Siq, where they could catch a glimpse of the monumental tomb known as the Khazneh (or "Treasury") before they entered the main civic area. In antiquity, the city was a prominent commercial centre, involved particularly in the manufacture of perfume, and was second in importance only to Bostra (present-day Busra in Syria), the capital of the Roman province of Arabia.

Ten years earlier than Bertou's visit, his fellow countryman Comte Léon de Laborde and his perennial companion, the engineer Louis Linant, had spent two or three days studying the ruins, in the course of which they found that one of the famous rock-cut tombs (fig. 8) carried a Latin inscription, "which is important, as it gives the name of a magistrate, Quintus Praetextus Florentinus, who died in this city while he was governor of this part of Arabia, and appears to date from the time of Hadrian or Antoninus Pius".[128] It was this inscription that Bertou had decided to transcribe and publish, as he was unable to resolve the weather-worn lettering of the opening line into the name quoted by Laborde.[129] Curiously, when

---

[127] The line is from John Burgon's poem *Petra* (1845), the source of the well-known phrase, "a rose-red city half as old as time".

[128] L. de Laborde & Linant, *Voyage de l'Arabie Pétrée* (Paris 1830), p. 59, with plate 46. Laborde did not include a detailed reading of the inscription.

[129] Bertou, *op. cit.* (n. 126), p. 30-31. Bertou's reading (MEMINTO EII PAI SEXTO FLORENTINO) was accepted by Th. Mommsen,

Figure 8: Tomb of Florentinus in Petra

Laborde finally published his erroneous reading of the inscription in 1847, he did not mention Bertou.[130]

Corpus Inscriptionum Latinarum Vol. 3: *Inscriptiones Asiae Provinciarum Europae Graecarum Illyrici Latinae*, Part 1 (Berlin 1873), p. 17, no. 87.

[130] L. de Laborde, "Inscriptions grecque et latine inédites trouvées en 1827 sur les façades de deux tombeaux dans les ruines de

However, it was less the man's name than his presence at Petra that drew him to Borghesi's attention, for he knew that any Roman official's presence in that city must postdate Trajan's conquest of Arabia in AD 106. Furthermore, he felt that the general absence of military decorations in Florentinus' career, as restored from Bertou's transcription, placed his governorship in the more peaceful time of Hadrian, rather than the later years of Trajan, "cluttered with wars". Thus, the inscription might supply valuable chronological markers for Borghesi's prosopographical technique.

The dating was important as, prior to his governorship of Arabia and a previous proconsulship of the province of Gallia Narbonensis (present-day Provence in southern France), Florentinus had served as *leg(atus) leg(ionis) VIIII Hisp(anae)* ("commander of the Ninth Hispana Legion"). But when exactly had his service in the Ninth Legion occurred?

The timely publication of a collection of inscriptions from the Rhineland, assembled by the lawyer and historian Johann Wilhelm Steiner,[131] gave Borghesi the opportunity to review the evidence for the various legions.[132] To try and clarify

---

Ouadi Mousa, l'ancienne capitale des Nabatæens", *Revue Archéologique* Vol. 1 (1847), pp. 253-260, at p. 258.

[131] J.W.C. Steiner, *Codex inscriptionum Romanorum Rheni*, 2 vols. (Darmstadt 1837).

[132] B. Borghesi, "Sull'opera intitolata *Codex Inscriptionum Romanarum Rheni* e sulle legioni che stanziarono nelle due Germanie da Tiberio fino a Gallieno", *Annali dell'Instituto di Corrispondenza Archeologica* Vol. 11 (1839), pp. 128-180, reprinted in *Oeuvres complètes de*

matters, he introduced another passage from the *Historia Augusta*, recording an anecdote in which the philosopher Favorinus was supposed to have deferred to the emperor Hadrian on a point of grammar, on the starkly pragmatic grounds that "the most learned of men is he who has thirty legions at his disposal".[133]

The arithmetic was straightforward. Borghesi counted thirty legions in existence on the eve of the Civil War of AD 69, and reasoned that, thereafter, new legions were only raised to replace any that were lost. Furthermore, when Trajan created the Thirtieth Ulpia Legion, it seemed logical to suppose that the name indicated that the total number of legions was thereby restored to thirty. Borghesi knew of five legions that had been lost in the intervening period, but only four that had been raised; so, by his reckoning, Trajan needed to create only one new legion to restore the total to thirty.

However, he was aware that Trajan, in fact, raised two legions: the Second Traiana and the Thirtieth Ulpia. Consequently, he had to identify another legion for destruction prior to the reign of Trajan. This was a problem that would perplex Pfitzner and Grotefend as well, for in the search for legions attested in the first century AD but not listed on the Antonine *NOMINA LEG(ionum)* pillar, there were three possible

---

Bartolomeo Borghesi Vol 4, *Oeuvres épigraphiques* 2 (Paris 1865), pp. 181-265.

[133] *Historia Augusta, Life of Hadrian* 15.12-13.

candidates: the Ninth Hispana, the Twenty-First Rapax, and the Twenty-Second Deiotariana.[134]

Borghesi, probably correctly, decided that the Twenty-First Rapax had been destroyed in AD 92, thus proving his theory that there were thirty legions in existence on Hadrian's accession. The corollary was, of course, that the Ninth Hispana was one of those thirty, and only perished later in the reign of Hadrian "on the occasion of the revolt mentioned by the *Historia Augusta* and even more so by Fronto".[135]

Borghesi was confident that the career of Florentinus supported this theory, although he was unable to assign a firm date to his command of the Ninth Legion, suggesting vaguely that it could not have occurred "before Trajan's empire had reached maturity".[136]

The opinions of Borghesi carried considerable weight amongst the new generation of scholars, including Joachim Marquardt, who in 1846 had taken over authorship of the projected multi-volume *Handbuch der römischen Alterthümer* ("Handbook of Roman Antiquities"), on the death of its creator, Wilhelm Adolph Becker. When he came to compose a brief history of the legions for the obligatory section on military affairs, he cited Borghesi as the authority for the fact that

---

[134] See above, p. 49.

[135] Borghesi, *op. cit.* (n. 132), p. 170 (repr., p. 250).

[136] Borghesi, *op. cit.* (n. 132), p. 171 (repr., p. 251). Grotefend, *op. cit.* (n. 70), p. 889, also took the career of Florentinus as a broad indicator that "the *IX Hispana* still existed under Trajan".

the Ninth Legion had gone by the time of Marcus Aurelius, having last been seen during the reign of Trajan.[137]

Marquardt's words might have been prophetic, appearing as they did in 1853, for only a year later, the discovery of the inscribed slab at York, the last known handiwork of the legion and precisely dated to the reign of Trajan, would prove them strictly correct. However, perhaps having belatedly realized that this was not quite what Borghesi had said, the statement was amended in the second edition to read "last seen under Hadrian".[138]

In the meantime, Bertou was not the last philologist to visit Petra. Nor was he the last to subject Florentinus' tomb to scholarly scrutiny. In fact, the Roman historian Alfred von Domaszewski and the Orientalist Rudolf Ernst Brünnow, on a visit to the ruined city in 1897 and again in 1898, pronounced it to be "once upon a time the finest of all the tombs in the necropolis of Petra".[139] Most importantly, they were able to bring greater clarity to the man's name, for the inscription was now seen to read *L(ucio) ANINIO L(uci) FIL(io) PAP(iria) SEXTIO FLORENTINO* ("to Lucius Aninius Sextius Florentinus, son of Lucius, of the Papiria voting tribe"), though the

---

[137] J. Marquardt, "Das Militärwesen", *Handbuch der römischen Alterthümer* Vol. 3, Part 2 (Leipzig 1853), pp. 235-479, at p. 356 n. 27.

[138] J. Marquardt, "Das Militärwesen", *Römische Staatsverwaltung* Vol. 2 (Leipzig 1876), pp. 309-591, at p. 436 n. 7.

[139] R.E. Brünnow & A. v. Domaszewski, *Die Provincia Arabia* Vol. 1 (Strassburg 1904), p. 169.

initial *L* was somewhat unclear.[140] But the date of his governorship remained elusive.

Here matters stood until 1961. In that year, the Israeli archaeologist Yigael Yadin, excavating the so-called Cave of Letters, located in the cliff face of Nahal Hever in the Judaean desert, uncovered an ancient cache of papyrus documents tied up in a leather bag. The documents, now known collectively as the "Babatha archive", were Greek, Aramaic, and Nabataean legal contracts dating from the period AD 93-132, all belonging to a Jewess of that name.

By good fortune, tucked away amongst the documents was a declaration of land ownership submitted to the Roman authorities on 2 December AD 127. In it, Babatha listed four orchards of date palms, located in the region administered from the city of Petra, "because a census of Arabia is being conducted by Titus Aninius Sextius Florentinus, *legatus Augusti pro praetore*".[141]

Another document from the same archive demonstrated that a different man, Titus Haterius Nepos, was governor on 17 November AD 130, so Florentinus had perhaps died earlier

---

[140] Brünnow & Domaszewski, *op. cit.* (n. 139), p. 382, no. 763, whence Th. Mommsen, O. Hirschfeld & A. Domaszewski, *Corpus Inscriptionum Latinarum* Vol. 3, *Inscriptionum Orientis et Illyrici Latinarum Supplementum* (Berlin 1902) Part 2, p. 2302, no. 14148[10].

[141] *P. Yadin* 16 = N. Lewis (ed.), *The Documents from the Bar Kokhba Period in the Cave of Letters: Greek Papyri* (Jerusalem 1989), pp. 65-70. First noted (as "Document 14") by Y. Yadin, "The Nabataean Kingdom, Provincia Arabia, Petra and En-Geddi in the documents from Nahal Hever", *Jaarbericht Ex Oriente Lux* Vol. 17 (1963), pp. 227-241.

that year or in the previous one.[142] A third document shows that Tiberius Julius Julianus Alexander was governor on 12 October AD 125, so we might tentatively suggest that Florentinus had arrived in the province in AD 126. If he had spent the previous three years as proconsul of Narbonensis, his command of the Ninth Legion would then have fallen around AD 120. With an average tenure of three years, we might even suppose that he had been the commander during Hadrian's visit to Britain in AD 122 and that his tribune might have been Lucius Aemilius Karus.

At any rate, while Borghesi's suggestion that the Ninth Legion had continued to exist into the reign of Hadrian gained further support from the Petra inscription, the career of a fourth senator was about to prove it beyond doubt. Sadly, if reports of this man's existence ever reached San Marino, Borghesi's untimely death in 1860 denied us knowledge of the great man's response.

---

[142] *P. Yadin* 23. Haterius Nepos is also named in *P. Yadin* 25 of 9 July AD 131.

6 THE PATRON OF TIMGAD

IN THE 1850S, while the Revd Wellbeloved was studying the meagre traces of the Roman occupation at York, 2000 km away to the south, another legionary fortress was giving up its secrets in abundance.

This was the fortress of the Third Augusta Legion at Lambaesis (present-day Tazoult-Lambèse in Algeria). Situated on a plateau in the northern foothills of the Aurès Mountains, the ruins of the fortress and surrounding town sprawled across 400 hectares. Untouched since antiquity, its abundant good quality building stone had attracted the attentions of a detachment of the French Foreign Legion, stationed at nearby Batna. They naturally exploited it as a quarry when, in 1850, they were ordered to build a penitentiary to house political prisoners, and it was doubly unfortunate that the construction of the prison obliterated around one-third of the fortress.

The ruins also inspired the regiment's Colonel, Jean-Luc Carbuccia, to engage in archaeological exploration, however rudimentary, and although the French military authorities were largely unsympathetic, contemporary scholars welcomed his efforts.[143]

One consequence of this exploration was that, in 1851 and 1852, Léon Renier, assistant librarian at the Sorbonne, was sent by the French Ministry of Public Education to study the epigraphic monuments of the area.[144] He was accompanied by Captain Adolphe Delamare, a veteran of the French government's scientific exploration of Algeria in the 1840s, who had already produced a volume of beautiful drawings depicting some of the antiquities of Algeria.[145] Sadly, his drawings of Lambaesis were never published.

Renier found the fortress in an astonishing state of preservation, compared with the examples he knew on the Rhine at Mainz, Bonn and Cologne, which had all been built upon by subsequent generations. (He might equally have included York in his list.) The ramparts, which enclosed a rectangular area of roughly 500m by 400m, still stood around 4m high, and the corner and interval towers could easily be distinguished. The south gate had already disappeared beneath the penitentiary building, but Renier recorded the other three,

---

[143] E.-F. Jomard, "Travail archéologique du colonel Carbuccia", *Mémoires de l'Institut impérial de France, Académie des inscriptions et belles-lettres* Vol. 18 (1855), pp. 161-170.

[144] His reports appeared in *Archives des missions scientifiques et littéraires* Vol. 2 (1851), pp. 169-186, 217-222, 435-457, and 473-483; Vol. 3 (1854), pp. 315-338.

[145] A.H.A. Delamare, *Exploration scientifique de l'Algérie: Archéologie* (Paris 1850).

along with the main roads issuing from them. At the centre of the fortress, straddling the point where the road from the north gate (the so-called *via praetoria*) met the road connecting the east and west gates (the *via principalis*), stood an imposing two-storey structure that he took to be the *praetorium*, or headquarters building. In fact, it is an example of a structure known as a *quadrifrons*, or four-faced arch, which was designed to sit on a cross roads. Its survival amid the ruins was remarkable, and Carbuccia's men had begun using it as a safe storage area for the sculpture and inscriptions they found.

Renier recorded no fewer than 1,478 inscriptions from the site.[146] These, he believed, "contained a wealth of information, which, gathered and studied, would produce results that fully justified the exercise".[147] A selection of 78 texts had already achieved inclusion in a publication jointly authored with Delamare prior to Renier's visit.[148] Others, newly discovered, were mentioned in his periodic reports.

However, it is curious that one inscription in particular drew no comment at the time. This was the dedication erected by veterans of the Third Augusta Legion to their commander, the *de facto* governor of Numidia, Lucius Novius Crispinus Martialis Saturninus, which listed his *cursus honorum* up until

---

[146] L. Renier, *Inscriptions romaines de l'Algérie* (Paris 1855). Additional fascicules were issued in subsequent years and the final publication appeared in 1886.

[147] Renier, *op. cit.* (n. 144), p. 170.

[148] A.H.A. De La Mare, *Recherches sur l'ancienne ville de Lambèse. Inscriptions antiques avec des notes explicatives par Léon Renier* (Paris 1850).

that point.[149] Renier noted its findspot as "north-east of the temple of Aesculapius", which lay around 1 km south-east of the fortress in an area explored by Carbuccia's men in 1849. By the mid-1870s, when Wilmanns was compiling the entries for *CIL* VIII, the inscription had been moved for safe keeping to the so-called *"praetorium"*.[150]

The dedication showed that, prior to Crispinus' entry into the senate, he had spent his vigintivirate as *quattuorvir viarum curandarum* (one of the four minor magistrates concerned with maintaining the streets of Rome), a post generally assumed to have provided a solid start for those seeking employment in the imperial service. He had also received the signal honour of presiding at the annual equestrian ceremony of the "Troy games" as a *sevir equitum Romanorum* (one of the six officials responsible for the games). But most importantly for us, he had served as *trib(unus) mil(itum) leg(ionis) VIIII Hisp(anae)* ("military tribune of the Ninth Hispana Legion").

The epigrapher Wilhelm Henzen seems to have been the first to notice this fact. He was one of several scholars who

---

[149] The stone (*CIL* VIII, 2747 = *ILS* 1070) was first reported in Renier, *op. cit.* (n. 146), p. 5, as no. 19. A similar dedication, reported by A. Poulle, "Nouvelles inscriptions de Thimgad, de Lambèse et de Marcouna", *Recueil des notices et mémoires de la Société archéologique de la province de Constantine* Vol. 22 (1882), pp. 331-406, at p. 387, no. 137, whence *CIL* VIII, 18273, appears to have been erected by officers of the legion.

[150] G. Wilmanns, *Corpus Inscriptionum Latinarum* Vol. 8, *Inscriptiones Africae Latinae* (Berlin 1881) Part 1, p. 325, no. 2747. He had earlier included it in his compendium, *op. cit.* (n. 6), Vol. 1, p. 388, no. 1185.

were invited to contribute annotations to the collected edition of Borghesi's works, a project sponsored by Napoléon III upon receiving news of the great scholar's death in 1860. In a note appended to Borghesi's remarks about Sextius Florentinus, Henzen wrote that "it follows from an inscription of Lambaesis that the IX *Hispanica* legion still existed under Hadrian".[151]

As Crispinus' tribunate was not securely dated, Henzen must have banked on the fact that a *leg(atus) Aug(usti) pr(o) pr(aetore) provinciae Africae* (the correct title for the praetorian official who commanded the emperor's forces inside the territory of Numidia) would have been a legionary tribune around twenty years earlier.

Crispinus' term of office in Africa was known to have spanned AD 147 and 148.[152] Henzen would have reasoned that, as a different man held the command in AD 146,[153] and as a *triennium* was common for such a post, Crispinus' term probably encompassed AD 149 as well. In fact, it was commonly believed that the previously mentioned dedication

---

[151] *Oeuvres complètes de Bartolomeo Borghesi* Vol. 4, *Oeuvres épigraphiques* 2 (Paris 1865), p. 251, n. 2.

[152] AD 147: *CIL* VIII, 2542 = Renier, *op. cit.* (n. 146), p. 5, no. 17. It was previously noted in 1850 by Renier in De La Mare, *op. cit.* (n. 148), p. 81, no. 23. It is evidently the same inscription as M. Besnier, "Inscriptions et monuments figures de Lambèse et de Tébessa", *Mélanges d'archéologie et d'histoire* Vol. 17 (1897), pp. 441-465, at pp. 441-444, no. 1, whence *AE* 1898, 11. AD 148: *CIL* VIII, 2652 = Renier, *op. cit.* (n. 146), p. 4, no. 18.

[153] Gaius Ulpius Messalinus: *CIL* VIII, 2536 = Renier, *op. cit.* (n. 146), p. 4, no. 11.

listing Crispinus' *cursus honorum* had been set up in AD 150, as the veterans responsible for it had enlisted in AD 124 and 125.[154] However, the arithmetic cannot be squared with the standard 26 years' service required of legionaries and the fact that discharges appear only to have been made every two years. In fact, as the epigrapher Clément Pallu de Lessert observed, an analogous inscription erected by the veterans of AD 152 and 153 appears to date from AD 176, at least two years prior to the likely date of their release.[155]

In passing, it is interesting to note that the veterans appear to have established their own quasi-religious association at Lambaesis, as Crispinus made dedications on behalf of two different members of the *curia Hadriana felix veteranorum leg(ionis) III Aug(ustae)* ("auspicious Hadrianic fraternity of veterans of the Third Augusta legion"), on the occasion of their elevation to the office of *flamen perpetuus* ("priest in perpetuity") (fig. 9).[156]

---

[154] This was the opinion of Wilmanns, *locc. citt.* (n. 150), repeated by (*e.g.*) H. Dessau, *Prosopographia Imperii Romani saeculorum I, II, III*, Vol. 2 (Berlin 1897), p. 417, no. N144.

[155] C. Pallu de Lessert, "Fastes de la Numidie sous la domination romaine", *Recueil des notices et mémoires de la Société archéologique de la province de Constantine* Vol. 25 (1888), pp. 1-261, at p. 72, citing *CIL* VIII, 2547 = Renier, *op. cit.* (n. 146), p. 9, no. 45.

[156] A. Poulle, "Nouvelles inscriptions de Lambèse et de Thimgad", *Recueil des notices et mémoires de la Société archéologique de la province de Constantine* Vol. 23 (1884), pp. 177-256, at p. 213, no. 3, whence *CIL* VIII, 18214 = *ILS* 6847. Poulle, *op. cit.* (n. 149), p. 366, no. 113, whence *CIL* VIII, 18234.

Figure 9: Dedication by Crispinus at Lambaesis

Although the prolongation of Crispinus' command into AD 150 appears to be unlikely, the previous year seemed assured by the surviving half of a monumental inscription discovered at the north gate of Thamugadi (Timgad in Algeria). This town, some 30 km from Lambaesis, was a Roman colony planted by Trajan in AD 100. The structure originally adorned by the inscription had been dedicated in AD 149, and although the dedicator's name was lost, the fact that he was *[co(n)s(ul)] design(atus) patronus col(oniae)* ("consul designate, patron of the colony") suggested Crispinus,[157] who is named as *patronus col(oniae)* on another dedication at Thamugadi.[158]

The supposition was confirmed in 1930, with the discovery of a similar dedication set up in AD 149 by Crispinus, *co(n)s(ul) designatus, patronus municipi(i)* ("consul designate, patron of the town"), at Diana Veteranorum (present-day Zana), 40 km north-west of Lambaesis.[159] It is quite likely, then, that the dedication by the veterans of the Third Augusta Legion was also erected in AD 149, as it, too, names Crispinus as *co(n)s(ul) desig(natus)*.[160]

The role of *patronus* of a town saddled the holder with great responsibility, which could only adequately be discharged by men of wealth and influence. Only a few years after Crispinus' departure, the orator Fronto wrote to the town

---

[157] A. Poulle, "Inscriptions diverses de la Numidie et de la Mauretanie Sétifienne", *Recueil des notices et mémoires de la Société archéologique de la province de Constantine* Vol. 25 (1888), pp. 400-434, at p. 407, no. 19, whence *CIL* VIII, 17852 = *AE* 1890, 75.

[158] A. Poulle, "Inscriptions diverses de la Numidie et de la Mauretanie Sétifienne", *Recueil des notices et mémoires de la Société archéologique de la province de Constantine* Vol. 24 (1886), pp. 139-198, at p. 154, no. 14, whence *CIL* VIII, 17894.

[159] R. Cagnat, "Séance de la Commission de l'Afrique du Nord", *Bulletin archéologique du comité des travaux historiques et scientifiques, 1930-1931* (1933), pp. 40-57, at pp. 51-52, whence *AE* 1930, 40.

[160] For Crispinus with the same title, *cf. CIL* VIII, 4199 = *ILS* 6850 = Renier, *op. cit.* (n. 146), p. 161, no. 1410 (from Verecunda, present-day Markouna, Algeria); 18083 = Poulle, *op. cit.* (n. 149), p. 386, n. 136.

council of his native Cirta (present-day Constantine in Algeria) to decline the honour of being their patron, on the grounds that the ideal candidates were "those who, at present, occupy the foremost position in public life".[161] Fronto would then have been around 60 years of age, whereas we can assume that Crispinus was barely 40.

Many of Crispinus' predecessors and successors in the Numidian command were likewise *patroni* of various towns in the neighbourhood of Lambaesis, where, like him, they can be seen to have dedicated public buildings. Also like him, on laying down their command, they expected to proceed directly to a consulship. The example of Titus Caesernius Statianus (a *Xvir stlitibus iudicandis* who appears not to have held a legionary tribunate, but skipped straight to a quaestorship as a candidate of Hadrian, whom he accompanied to the east in AD 128) may smack of imperial favouritism, but illustrates the process. Caesernius appears as *leg(atus) Aug(usti) pro pr(aetore) co(n)s(ul) desig(natus)* on much-damaged dedications of AD 140 found at Diana Veteranorum and Gemellae (present-day El-Kasbat in Algeria) and another of AD 141 from Thamugadi,[162] and is already named as consul on a dedication

---

[161] Fronto, *Letters to his Friends* 2.10 = Naber, *op. cit.* (n. 111), pp. 200-201.

[162] *AE* 1930, 39 (Zana); 1950, 60 (El-Kasbat); 1985, 874 + *CIL* VIII, 2361 = 17849 (Timgad). He was presumably patron of these towns. *AE* 1954, 150 names him as *patronus coloniae* at Timgad.

erected at Cirta *p(ecunia) p(ublica)* ("at public expense") in AD 141.[163]

If further proof is needed, Crispinus' predecessor, Gaius Ulpius Pacatus Prastina Messalinus, will suffice. Known to have held the Numidian command in AD 143,[164] he was still in post in AD 145, according to a dedication by a vexillation of the Sixth Ferrata Legion, which was building a road in the Aurès Mountains in that year.[165] Although an inscription of AD 146 names him simply as *leg(atus) Aug(usti) pro pr(aetore) leg(ionis) III Aug(ustae)*,[166] the title *co(n)s(ul) desig(natus)* is added on a pair of monumental dedications from Thamugadi, probably erected in that same year, honouring him *universum opus perductionis aquae inchoatum et consummatum* ("for having begun and completed the entire waterworks").[167] He was one of the *consules ordinarii* in AD 147.[168]

Consequently, scholars have generally assumed that Crispinus was consul in AD 150.[169] He would then have been born around AD 110, so that his legionary tribunate could not

---

[163] *CIL* VIII, 7036 = *ILS* 1068, which gives his career up to the consulship. *AE* 2002, 1147 confirms his consulship in AD 141.

[164] *AE* 1902, 146 = *CIL* VIII, 17851 + 17860, naming him as patron of Timgad.

[165] *CIL* VIII, 10230 = *ILS* 2479.

[166] *CIL* VIII, 2536.

[167] *AE* 1985, 875a and b. The title also appears on *CIL* VIII, 17723 (undated).

[168] *AE* 1904, 218; *CIL* IX, 4957.

[169] E.g. Dessau, *loc. cit.* (n. 154). Only C. Pallu de Lessert, *Fastes des provinces Africaines* Vol. 1 (Paris 1896), p. 364, canvassed the possibility that his consulship may have occurred late in AD 149.

reasonably be placed any earlier than AD 128. Henzen was presumably thinking along these lines when he wrote his laconic note.

With the appearance of this new evidence, Borghesi's belief that there were Hadrianic senators who had served with the Ninth Legion was triumphantly vindicated. Nevertheless, like Grotefend, he saw no reason to doubt that the legion had suffered some catastrophe in Hadrianic Britain, although Hübner felt compelled to embellish the theory, when he wrote in 1873 that, "since it is agreed that the Ninth Legion was not taken to another province, it is not improbable, as Borghesi inferred from the testimony of the *Historia Augusta* and Fronto, that it was destroyed in Britain by the Brigantes".[170]

---

[170] Hübner, *op. cit.* (n. 42), p. 64. Borghesi had not mentioned the Brigantes.

7 PICTS, SCOTS, AND BRIGANTES

UNBEKNOWN TO BORGHESI, his prosopographical ambitions were preparing the way for one of the giants of Roman history. In 1845 and again in 1847, Theodor Mommsen, travelling in Italy on a scholarship from the Danish government, visited the Count of San Marino, following in the footsteps of other scholars who were then scouring Italy for Roman inscriptions – notably the Dane Olaus Kellermann in 1835 and Wilhelm Henzen, a close contemporary of Mommsen's, in 1844.

Some years later, while briefly holding a professorship in Roman Law at Zurich (before finally securing a sought-after position in Berlin), Mommsen published the fruits of his sojourn in Italy: a catalogue of the Latin inscriptions from the territory of the Kingdom of Naples, which he had assembled at Borghesi's urging. The volume was appropriately dedicated "to Bartolomeo Borghesi, teacher, patron, friend".[171]

This volume, and a subsequent one gathering the Roman inscriptions of Switzerland,[172] gave a foretaste of Mommsen's vision for the *Corpus Inscriptionum Latinarum* project, with inscriptions systematically arranged by town or territory, and a prefatory list of antiquarian sources consulted.

Over the course of the next fifty years, until his death in 1903, Mommsen worked tirelessly on matters of Roman history. By 1856, he had already completed his *Römische Geschichte* ("History of Rome") in three volumes, for which he was belatedly awarded the Nobel Prize in Literature in 1902. A fourth volume, continuing the story beyond 46 BC, was occasionally mentioned but never embarked upon, although he frequently lectured on the "History of Rome under the Emperors" until the age of 70.

Finally, in 1885, a new volume appeared, ostensibly the fifth, entitled *Die Provinzen von Caesar bis Diocletian* ("The Provinces from Caesar to Diocletian"). Here Mommsen attempted to deploy the knowledge gleaned from the ongoing *CIL* project to present a military history of the Roman empire, province by province. It was hailed by one contemporary as "a stupendous work".[173]

---

[171] Th. Mommsen, *Inscriptiones Regni Neapolitani Latinae* (Leipzig 1852).

[172] Th. Mommsen, *Inscriptiones Confoederationis Helveticae Latinae* (*Mitteilungen der antiquarischen Gesellschaft in Zürich* Vol. 10, 1854).

[173] F. Haverfield, "Theodor Mommsen", *The English Historical Review* Vol. 19, no. 73 (1904), pp. 80-89, at p. 85.

If the chapter dealing with Britain was felt by contemporaries to be weak, it was largely on account of its brevity and was no reflection of its content. But it is surprising to learn that Mommsen boldly lent his considerable authority to the theory that, "under Hadrian, there was a terrible catastrophe here, apparently an attack on the fortress at Eburacum and the annihilation of the legion stationed there, the very same Ninth that had fought so unluckily in the Boudiccan revolt".[174]

The discovery of the York inscription in 1854, and more particularly Hübner's inclusion of it in *CIL* VII in 1873,[175] had enabled Mommsen to narrow the chronology somewhat, because it proved that the Ninth Legion was actively building there during Trajan's reign. Thus, he announced that the disaster had occurred "undoubtedly soon after AD 108", adding that "this was probably not caused by an enemy invasion, but rather by a revolt of the northern allied peoples, particularly the Brigantes".

Though hailed as a "brilliant conjecture" by one reviewer,[176] another preferred caution, conceding that "the conjecture is bold, though perhaps acceptable", while pointing out that "when we separate hypothesis from facts, we do not know more than that the inscriptions of the Ninth Legion

---

[174] Th. Mommsen, *Römische Geschichte* Vol. 5. *Die Provinzen von Caesar bis Diocletian* (Berlin 1885), p. 171.

[175] See *supra*, n. 42. It had not achieved inclusion in the Revd J. McCaul's *Britanno-Roman Inscriptions* (London 1863).

[176] T.F. Tout, *English Historical Review* Vol. 1, no. 2 (1886), pp. 361-364, at p. 362.

suddenly end".[177] However, it is difficult to see why Mommsen's contemporaries found the hypothesis acceptable. Leaving aside the puzzle of how a disaster under Hadrian could have occurred "soon after AD 108", where was the evidence of an attack on the fortress at York by the neighbouring Brigantes?

The tribe of the Brigantes, "said to be the most populous in the whole province",[178] occupied a huge swathe of lands from the River Humber right up to the River Tyne. Following their conquest in the early AD 70s and the establishing of a legionary fortress in their midst at York, they appear to have remained passive and peaceful. It seems that Mommsen's justification for accusing them of revolt stemmed from his reading of Juvenal's satire on setting a parental example, in which the poet recommends (tongue in cheek) that the boy who covets a successful military career must be sure to "demolish the huts of the Moors and the forts of the Brigantes".[179]

Although the few allusions to Britain in Juvenal's work are normally linked with the Flavian conquest of northern England, this particular line had been quoted by the venerable Elizabethan antiquarian William Camden in the context of Hadrian's visit.[180] Hübner had certainly consulted Camden's *Britannia*, for every editor involved in the *Corpus Inscriptionum*

---

[177] F.T. Richards, "The new volume of Mommsen's History of Rome", *The Academy* Vol. 28 (1885), no. 701, pp. 231-232.
[178] Tac., *Agr.* 17.1.
[179] Juvenal, *Satires* 14.196.
[180] W. Camden, *Britannia* (London 1590), p. 554.

Latinarum project was obliged to trawl through all the previous publications of note concerning the antiquity of his allotted province. So it is quite likely that his reading of Camden influenced him to lay the charge of revolt on the Brigantes, though he swithered over the dating.[181] Mommsen, in turn, will have picked up the reference from Hübner. Yet this was a fragile peg on which to hang such a weighty theory, and one which – bearing the imprimatur of Mommsen – has echoed down through the generations.

Mommsen's reasoning was also founded upon his observation that "Hadrian's Wall presents a front towards the south as well as towards the north; evidently it was also intended to suppress the superficially subdued northern England".[182]

By coincidence, in the same year as *Die Provinzen von Caesar bis Diocletian* appeared, the Revd John Collingwood Bruce published the third edition of his *Hand-book to the Roman Wall*,[183] a *vade mecum* for the intrepid sightseer investigating

---

[181] See *supra*, p. 80 and n. 170. On the varying date: E. Hübner, "Britanni", *Paulys Real-Encyclopädie* Vol. 3.1 (1897), cols. 858-879, at col. 872: "The disappearance of the Ninth Legion under Trajan ... demonstrates continued fighting in the north"; *cf. idem*, "Das römische Heer in Britannien", *Hermes* Vol. 16 (1881), pp. 513-84, at p. 536: "Under Trajan or Hadrian, it seems that it met its end in battle with the Brigantes".

[182] Mommsen, *op. cit.* (n. 174), p. 172.

[183] Mommsen evidently knew the book's precursor, *The Roman Wall. A description of the mural barrier of the North of England* (3rd edn. London 1867), which is the only secondary source cited by him for information on Roman Britain.

the remains of Hadrian's Wall. In it, he described the great fortification running from Wallsend on the Tyne to Bowness on the Solway, comprising a stone wall fronted by a ditch on its northern side and accompanied by an earthen bank, the so-called Vallum, to the south. For a statement of its purpose, Bruce deferred to the opinion of Horsley, writing 150 years earlier. To both scholars, it seemed obvious that "whilst the Wall undertook the harder duty of warding off the professedly hostile tribes of Caledonia, the Vallum was intended as a protection against sudden surprise from the south. ... The natives of the country on the south side of the Wall, though conquered, were not to be depended upon; in the event of their kinsmen in the north gaining an advantage, they would be ready to avail themselves of it".[184]

Within a generation, scholars were taking exception to this view. In an appendix to the 1909 reprint of *The Provinces of the Roman Empire* (the authorized translation of Mommsen's *Provinzen*), Francis Haverfield, Camden Professor of Ancient History at Oxford and sometime correspondent of Mommsen's on matters epigraphic, pointed out that "the Vallum cannot be regarded as a military work",[185] on account of its non-defensive design. But although scholars now reject the

---

[184] J.C. Bruce, *The Hand-book to the Roman Wall* (3rd edn. London 1885), p. 23, citing Horsley, *op. cit.* (n. 47), p. 125.

[185] Th. Mommsen, *The Provinces of the Roman Empire from Caesar to Diocletian*, translated by W.P. Dickson (London 1886; corrected repr. 1909), Vol. 2, p. 351.

interpretation of the Vallum championed by Horsley and Bruce,[186] it would prove far more difficult to squeeze the genie of a Brigantian revolt back into the bottle from which Mommsen had released it.

It is all the more curious that Mommsen chose to enshrine this theory for all time in his *Römische Geschichte*, when we consider that he evidently told a different story to those who attended his Berlin University lectures. According to the transcript of Mommsen's 1883 lecture series on the Roman emperors from Vespasian to Diocletian, made by Sebastian Hensel (nephew of the composer Mendelssohn and father of Mommsen's student Paul Hensel):[187]

> A severe catastrophe must have occurred under the following [*viz.* Hadrianic] regime. We read of a great uprising of the Britons. Fronto, under the emperor Marcus, speaks of the huge number of soldiers who fell in Britain during Hadrian's rule. What is more – and this speaks more eloquently than any written account – the Ninth Legion, stationed at Eburacum, disappeared entirely and was not renewed. Some catastrophe must have occurred similar to that of Varus in the Teutoburg Forest.

---

[186] The passage in Bruce's *Handbook to the Roman Wall* was extensively redrafted by Collingwood, *op. cit.* (n. 47), 20, and the spirit, if not always the wording, of his version has been retained by subsequent editors.

[187] Th. Mommsen, *A History of Rome under the Emperors. Based on the lecture notes of Sebastian and Paul Hensel, 1882-6* (London 1996), p. 261.

> It was Roman custom not to re-establish under the same name a legion annihilated in this way. This was the case with the legions wiped out in the Teutoburg Forest and so also with the Ninth Legion, which was exposed to attacks from the Picts and Scots. But we have no details about this catastrophe, which occurred some time around 120.

The dating of AD 120 at least took the catastrophe into the reign of Hadrian, but it is more difficult to excuse Mommsen's identification of the culprits as "Picts and Scots", terms which scholars of the day knew to be anachronistic.[188] Finally, having described Hadrian's Wall and the Antonine Wall with broad brush strokes for his audience's benefit, Mommsen drew the conclusion that "these structures evidently stood in a causal relationship with the military events associated with the destruction of the camp at York and of the Ninth Legion".[189] However, it is unfortunate that he never divulged where his idea of destruction at York had come from, for there was no reason then (nor any reason now) to suggest such a thing.

---

[188] *E.g.*, Bruce, *op. cit.* (n. 183, a work consulted by Mommsen), p. 33, mentions them only from AD 368.

[189] Mommsen, *op. cit.* (n. 187), p. 262.

8 THE BROKEN EAGLE

MOMMSEN CAN PERHAPS be excused for his ignorance of archaeology, for that particular science was still in its infancy during his lifetime; in any case, it was not until the early twentieth century that Roman York was subjected to systematic excavation.

During the nineteenth century, Roman remains, wherever they were found, were invariably cleared out to reveal whatever stone structures still survived. For example, the Revd John Hodgson's investigation of the Roman fort at Housesteads on Hadrian's Wall in 1833, during which "the eastern gateway was totally freed from rubbish", was characterized by him as "houking", and it is noticeable that the "Mithraic antiquities" turned up by workmen ten years earlier excited more curiosity than the history of the fort itself.[190]

---

[190] J. Hodgson, *History of Northumberland*, Part II, Vol. III (Newcastle 1840), pp. 186-187 for the fort at Housesteads, and pp. 188-194 for the Mithraeum and associated speculations. R.C. Bosanquet, "Excavations on the line of the Roman Wall in Northumberland. The

In a continuation of the practices of earlier generations in search of Roman inscriptions, workmen were employed to do the spadework at such sites, there being no need for particular skill or technique. For example, while planning to investigate the Austrian site of Halstatt in 1866, the antiquarian Sir John Evans (father of the better known Arthur Evans, excavator of Minoan Crete) made preparations that were entirely characteristic of the day; as he informed his wife in a letter, "we arranged to set some men at work digging and are going up there early tomorrow morning to see the result".[191]

Although self-styled archaeological societies abounded in nineteenth-century Britain, they appear to have preferred social activities to practical ones. In 1857, Baron Talbot de Malahide addressed the annual meeting of the Royal Archaeological Institute as President, advising the members that "the business of the Institute must not be confined to the study of archaeology by means of hospitable entertainments, however pleasant to many that course might be, but the scientific department, however dry or tedious, should be strictly followed up".[192]

For many, the focus was the establishment of museums to house the burgeoning antiquarian collections of inscriptions,

---

Roman camp at Housesteads", *Archaeologia Aeliana*² Vol. 25 (1904), pp. 193-300, preserves the remark about "houking" on p. 200.

[191] Quoted in J. Evans, *Time and Chance. The Story of Arthur Evans and his Forebears* (London 1943), p. 122.

[192] "Annual Meeting, 1857, held at Chester", *The Archaeological Journal* Vol. 14 (1857), pp. 364-386, at p. 369.

coins, and domestic objects turned up by Victorian labourers and often only handed over on payment of a fee.

It is particularly telling that a contemporary guide to the archaeological antiquities of Britain devoted 15 pages, under the Romano-British heading, to inscriptions of various sorts, and a mere 2½ pages to "amphitheatres, stations, camps and roads" and a single page on "villas".[193]

However, organized excavation campaigns were occasionally funded by wealthy patrons. For example, Algernon Percy, 4th Duke of Northumberland, had been supportive of Bruce's work along Hadrian's Wall, and Arthur Wellesley, 2nd Duke of Wellington, on whose Hampshire estates lay Calleva, the ancient city of Silchester, was similarly inclined.

At this latter site, Camden recorded in 1590 that "nothing now remains but the walls which, stripped of their breastwork and battlements, seem to have been of great height".[194] Its 100-acre interior, an irregular octagon in shape, had been given over entirely to farmland, with the Manor Farm and parish church the only upstanding buildings. Over the years, antiquarians had occasionally investigated wherever the plough had struck masonry, but usually only to supplement their collections, in an age when artefacts were acquired as curiosities by the wealthy. It is typical of the times that, of the four inscriptions registered by Hübner as deriving from Calleva, the whereabouts of two could no longer be discover-

---

[193] J.Y. Akerman, *An Archaeological Index to Remains of Antiquity of the Celtic, Romano-British, and Anglo-Saxon Periods* (London 1847).

[194] Camden, *op. cit.* (n. 180), p. 201.

ed, though one of them had allegedly been carted off to Cambridge, and a third had arrived in that town by way of London.[195]

More intriguingly, it had been observed, from as long ago as the days of Camden, that in a dry summer the street layout of the buried town became visible in the fields, "for though the soil is rich and fertile enough, nevertheless in certain beds that intersect, the crop does not thrive in the same way, but is less dense than elsewhere, and along these the streets of the ancient city are thought to have run".[196]

Thus, in 1864, the site seemed worthy of exploration to the Duke, who had lately acquired a collection of artefacts gathered from its environs. The Revd James Joyce, with only a dilettante's knowledge of Pompeii to recommend him and four workmen to assist him, was engaged to direct the excavations, and over the next twenty years made a great success of the enterprise.

Joyce's uncovering of several town houses, with beautifully tiled floors and hypocausts, and his discovery of the central forum and basilica, the first to be revealed in Britain, amply justified the title of "Pompeii of England", presciently bestowed on the town by the antiquarian Henry Lawes Long

---

[195] Hübner, *op. cit.* (n. 42), p. 16, nos. 6-9, now *RIB* 67, 68, 87, and 72.

[196] Camden, *op. cit.* (n. 180), p. 202. The same phenomenon was observed by J. Ward, "A description of the town of Silchester in its present state", *Philosophical Transactions* Vol. 45, no. 490 (1748), pp. 603-614.

many years before Mommsen applied it to Wroxeter.[197] And it is to Joyce's great credit that, unusually amongst his contemporaries, he was sensitive to the possibility, not only of stratification, but also of using coin finds to broadly date those strata.

One discovery above all briefly caught the public imagination. In October 1866, while excavating the great basilica that formed one side of the forum, Joyce came upon the small bronze figurine of an eagle, some 6" (15cm) in height, buried beneath a thick layer of burnt debris and resting upon a surface marked by dark streaks, which Joyce took to be the charred remains of ceiling beams (fig. 10). This scene immediately conjured in the excavator's mind the episode of the short-lived usurpation of Carausius, who seized control of Britain in AD 286, and his successor, Allectus, who was finally defeated somewhere in Hampshire ten years later by the legitimate forces of Rome under Constantius, father of Constantine the Great.

Joyce evoked the romantic image of a rebel legionary eagle-bearer, beleaguered in the basilica as the liberating army closed in, wrenching as a last resort the sacred eagle from its staff and concealing it in the rafters, where it remained until the town's final destruction.[198] Naturally, the eagle became the

---

[197] H.L. Long, *Observations upon Certain Roman Roads and Towns in the South of Britain* (Farnham 1836), p. 3; *cf.* Mommsen, *op. cit.* (n. 174), p. 162 n. 1.

[198] J.G. Joyce, "The excavations at Silchester", *Archaeological Journal* Vol. 30 (1873), pp. 10-27, at pp. 25-6; "Third account of

centrepiece of Joyce's subsequent lectures and presentations, as one contemporary newspaper report shows:[199]

> Mr Joyce expatiated with glowing pride upon the value of this almost sacred object, and after picturing the bearer of the cohort standard as the most muscular and stalwart of Roman soldiers, chosen for the dangerous duty for his bravery and valour, and wearing the distinguishing lion's skin drawn over his head, he then eloquently painted the reverential bearing of the high-born tribune, to whom the inestimable legionary standard was entrusted as standing, bare-headed and uncovered at the sacrifices before the battle, with the standards of the cohorts in rank behind encompassing the Imperial eagle; and then as frantically, during some desperate struggle, tearing away the eagle from its staff, wrenching off the golden wings and concealing the high-prized body and its fragments amongst the timbers of the roof to save them from capture.

News of the discovery travelled far and wide. At a meeting of the Glasgow Archaeological Society on 16 December 1867, John Buchanan, a local banker whom Bruce nicknamed "the

---

excavations at Silchester", *Archaeologia* Vol. 46 (1881), pp. 344-365, at pp. 363-4.
[199] *The London Standard*, 10 August 1872.

Figure 10: The Silchester eagle

guardian genius of the Northern Wall" (referring to the Antonine Wall),[200] gave his audience "a rapid glimpse into the dark past":[201]

> The theory is that the town [of Silchester] had been burnt after a desperate struggle between the Romans there posted, and an enemy, and that the soldiers had to flee for their lives, before doing which they tore off the vertically raised wings of the eagle, the better to get the eagle itself hid in the roof of the court-house, which was probably guarded by the Romans, and formed the point where they made their last stand. ...

---

[200] J.C. Bruce, "The Antonine Wall", *Proceedings of the Society of Antiquaries of Newcastle-upon-Tyne* Vol. 1, no. 21 (1856), pp. 182-185, at p. 185.

[201] J. Buchanan, "Recent discovery of a Roman inscription near Glasgow", *Transactions of the Glasgow Archaeological Society* Vol. 2, no. 1 (1870), pp. 11-28, at pp. 24-5.

> There must have been a very bloody engagement at Silchester, of which we have no historical record, before the chosen cohort relinquished that sacred standard which was entrusted to their protection.

This was too good a story to be told only once. Buchanan accordingly reprised it a year later, reminding his audience of

> the discovery of the eagle of a Legion, in the ruins of the Roman City of Silchester, with the wings torn off, and exhibiting other indications of violence. From the great care taken by each Legion of this, its chief standard, which the soldiers were sworn to protect to the uttermost, a desperate struggle must have taken place before this Silchester eagle was left, leading, indeed, to the inference that an entire Legion, or at all events the milliary cohort which had the special custody of its eagle, had been cut to pieces.[202]

Popular books continued to mention the eagle as a relic of the fall of Silchester,[203] but within a generation it had faded from memory. Francis Haverfield, the pre-eminent Romano-British scholar of the day, scarcely mentioned such a singular find: it is entirely absent from his entry on Silchester, written for the new *Encyclopædia Britannica*,[204] and in his chapter on Romano-

---

[202] J. Buchanan, "Address to the Glasgow Archaeological Society, at its Annual Meeting on 2nd February, 1869", *Transactions of the Glasgow Archaeological Society* Vol. 2, no. 1 (1870), pp. 66-77, at p. 76.

[203] *E.g.* J.R. Green, *The Making of England* (London 1881), p. 116.

[204] F.J. Haverfield, "Silchester", *Encyclopædia Britannica*[10] Vol. 32 (London 1902), pp. 625-627.

British Hampshire for the Victoria County History, he simply noted that "no military objects have ever been found at Silchester except, perhaps, an eagle and a bit of inscribed bronze, and these are not necessarily of military origin".[205] (The inscribed bronze was, in fact, military, being one element of a now well-known type of tripartite belt-fitting set common in the early third century AD.)

By then, the eagle had found a home at Apsley House, the London residence of the Dukes of Wellington, for it was there that the Hampshire Field Club viewed it during their visit on 7 May 1913.[206] It was subsequently moved to the Dukes' country seat at Stratfieldsaye House, where a later generation of the Field Club were delighted to see it on 31 July 1945.[207] But it seems not to have aroused any particular scholarly interest in the meantime.

The eagle was finally purchased in 1980 by Reading Museum and Art Gallery, with the aid of grants from the Victoria & Albert Museum and the National Art Collections Fund. But a replica had been on display since 1949, thanks to the efforts

---

[205] F.J. Haverfield, "Romano-British Hampshire", in H.A. Doubleday (ed.), *The Victoria History of the Counties of England. Hampshire and the Isle of Wight* Vol. 1 (Westminster 1900), pp. 265-349, at p. 276 n. 3.

[206] W. Dale, "Excursion to Apsley House and Southwark Cathedral", *Papers and Proceedings of the Hampshire Field Club and Archaeological Society* Vol. 7 no. 1 (1914), pp. xxvii-xxxvii, at p. xxix.

[207] Anon, "Visit to Stratfieldsaye", *Papers and Proceedings of the Hampshire Field Club and Archaeological Society* Vol. 16 no. 3 (1947), p. 312.

of Councillor George W. Willis, founder of Basingstoke Museum. It was this replica that inspired the novelist Rosemary Sutcliff to write *The Eagle of the Ninth*. She informed her readers that "different people have had different ideas as to how it came to be there [*i.e.* at Silchester], but no one knows, just as no one knows what happened to the Ninth Legion after it marched into the northern mists".[208]

It was Sutcliff's idea to associate the eagle with the Ninth Legion when she decided to fashion her tale "from these two mysteries, brought together", but Joyce's interpretation of the figurine as a legionary standard, an interpretation upon which Sutcliff's story relied, had not gone unchallenged.

In 1950, when M.R. Hull, curator of Colchester Museum, included the replica eagle in an exhibition of artefacts to celebrate the town's nineteenth centenary, he described it as "perhaps from the head of the military standard, but may be from the decorations of the Forum or Basilica".[209] The archaeologist George Boon, who was then working as an assistant in Reading Museum, came down firmly in favour of the latter interpretation, writing that "the best suggestion is that it formed an adjunct of a larger bronze statue, perhaps being held in the hand, and certainly being more or less free-standing".[210] His view found favour with the foremost expert on Roman art in

---

[208] R. Sutcliff, *The Eagle of the Ninth* (Oxford 1954), foreword.

[209] M.R. Hull, *Catalogue of an exhibition of Romano-British antiquities* (Colchester 1950), p. 16, no. 39.

[210] G.C. Boon, *Roman Silchester. The Archaeology of a Romano-British Town* (London 1957), p. 100.

Britain, who observed that "the curve of the under sides of the feet suggest that the claws once clasped the surface of a globe; and indeed the most likely theory of the eagle's purpose is that it was the attribute held on a globe on the hand of a bronze statue, of Jupiter or of an Emperor".[211] She assigned its dating to the second century AD.

As for the circumstances of its deposition, Joyce's theory suffered a fatal blow in 1977, when, prior to the commencement of a major excavation campaign across the site of the forum and basilica, archaeologists reinvestigated the eagle's last resting place.[212] Joyce had shown that the basilica had been rebuilt at some point in its history, and for a long time, this second phase was characterized as a "barbarous rebuilding" after the destruction of the Carausian interlude.[213] However, the new excavations established that an original timber basilica of Flavian date had been dismantled and rebuilt in masonry, probably during the reign of Antoninus Pius, and that, by around the mid-third century, the basilica was no longer in use and the site had been given over to iron-working activities. The corner room where the eagle was found seemed to have experienced a slightly different course of events. The dark streaks that Joyce discerned beneath the eagle were

---

[211] J.M.C. Toynbee, *Art in Roman Britain* (London 1962), p. 150, no. 60.

[212] M. Fulford & J. Timby, *Late Iron Age and Roman Silchester. Excavations on the site of the forum-basilica 1977, 1980-86* (London 2000), esp. pp. 67-68 and 75.

[213] G.E. Fox, "Silchester", *The Archaeological Journal* Vol. 51 (1894), pp. 337-359, at p. 354; *cf.* Boon, *op. cit.* (n. 210), pp. 90-100.

reinterpreted as the floor joists laid during the construction of the original timber basilica, and the burnt layer that sealed the whole deposit would then belong to the demolition that preceded the construction of the masonry basilica. Any items recovered from this context would then have been lost prior to around AD 150, far earlier than Joyce's preferred scenario.

Nevertheless, it was this romantic tale of a legionary eagle concealed for safe-keeping in the roof-space of the basilica and subsequently lost in its third-century destruction that Sutcliff wove into her sequel.[214] In reality, of course, the events at Silchester were entirely divorced from the history of the Ninth Legion.

---

[214] R. Sutcliff, *The Silver Branch* (Oxford 1957).

9 IN MOMMSEN'S SHADOW

BY THE TURN OF THE CENTURY, two generations of scholars had grown up with Mommsen's *Römische Geschichte* and were hard at work crafting their own Roman histories. However, it is evident that they struggled to escape from Mommsen's shadow.

The archaeologist and historian Alfred von Domaszewski's version of events, for example, seemed to owe more to Mommsen's *Provinzen* than to the primary sources. Domaszewski had just seen the three-volume *Die Provincia Arabia* through the press, the first volume of which had featured the tomb of Sextius Florentinus, one-time commander of the Ninth Legion.[215] But of course, no date could yet be assigned to his career. When Dessau added him to the *Prosopographia Imperii Romani*, he could only suggest, rather vagu-

---

[215] See *supra*, n. 139.

ely, that "it seems that Florentinus did not live after Hadrian, in whose time the Ninth Hispana Legion perished".[216]

Consequently, Domaszewski saw no reason to doubt Mommsen's version, which he essentially summarized in his statement that "Hadrian went to Britain, where a major uprising, in which the Ninth Legion had met with its destruction, had been suppressed".[217] Sadly, as his *Geschichte der römischen Kaiser* ("History of the Roman Emperors") was conceived for "the cultured public", rather than for students or scholars, he skated over such matters in a very superficial way. In an earlier work, he had likewise informed his readers that "the *legio IX Hispana* probably perished under Hadrian".[218]

English historians were also in thrall to Mommsen. Francis Haverfield, who had carried on a long correspondence with Mommsen and had even managed to eclipse Hübner in matters of Romano-British epigraphy, naturally repeated Mommsen's version of events when he delivered the prestigious Ford Lectures in 1907: "late in the reign of Trajan or early in that of Hadrian ... The north rose and not in vain. The Ninth Legion, then stationed at York, was annihilated. The rising was, of course, crushed".[219] Haverfield dated the event

---

[216] Dessau, *op. cit.* (n. 154), p. 84, no. F300.

[217] A. von Domaszewski, *Geschichte der römischen Kaiser* (Leipzig 1909) Vol. 2, p. 194. The only chronological indicator he provided was that Hadrian then left Britain in AD 122.

[218] A. von Domaszewski, *Die Fahnen im römischen Heere* (Vienna 1885), p. 37 n. 2.

[219] F.G. Haverfield, *The Roman Occupation of Britain* (ed. G. Macdonald, Oxford 1924), p. 119.

broadly to AD 115-120.[220] Likewise, successive editions of Sir Charles Oman's *England before the Norman Conquest* repeated the statement that the Ninth Legion "must have been exterminated in some unrecorded Brigantian battle",[221] referring the reader to Mommsen's *Roman History* for details, while as late as 1923, the Roman historian B.W. Henderson, writing about Hadrian's visit, informed his readers that "the Brigantes of Yorkshire had risen but a few years since and had cut one unlucky legion, the Ninth, to pieces".[222]

In the meantime, Wilhelm Weber, one of Domaszewski's students, had published a very detailed study of Hadrian's reign, based on his doctoral thesis. In it, he, too, accepted Mommsen's version, simply pointing out that "the views of scholars fluctuate regarding the date of the uprising".[223] Clearly, this uprising and the consequent destruction of the legion were not in question; only the timing. He decided upon AD 119/120, based on the evidence of Hadrian's *BRITANNIA* and *EXPED(itio) AUG(usti)* ("imperial expedition") coins,

---

[220] F.G. Haverfield, "Roman Britain", *Encyclopædia Britannica*[11] Vol. 4 (Cambridge 1910), pp. 583-589, at p. 584; "Roman Britain", *The Cambridge Medieval History* Vol. 1 (Cambridge 1911), pp. 367-381, at p. 368.

[221] C. Oman, *England before the Norman Conquest* (London 1910; 8th edn. 1938), p. 110; cf. p. 109, n. 2: "probably it was destroyed in AD 119".

[222] B.W. Henderson, *The Life and Principate of the Emperor Hadrian AD 76-138* (London 1923), p. 79, adding that "the Brigantes' rising is usually set in AD 117" (n. 1).

[223] W. Weber, *Untersuchungen zur Geschichte des Kaisers Hadrianus* (Leipzig 1907), p. 109.

Figure 11: Hadrian's titulature on the coinage

which indicated a punitive campaign to crush the insurgent tribes into obedience.[224]

However, Hadrian's coinage is notoriously difficult to date; whereas many emperors' titulature changed from year to year, Hadrian resolutely remained simply *CO(n)S(ul) III* ("three-times consul") from AD 119 until his death in AD 138, only adding *P(ater) P(atriae)* ("father of his country") from AD 128 onwards (fig. 11). Thus, although the coin expert Harold Mattingly placed the *BRITANNIA* coin in AD 119 and the *EXPED(itio) AUG(usti)* coin in AD 121, his reasoning was entirely subjective, and there was no reason why both should not commemorate the emperor's visit in AD 122.[225]

---

[224] Weber, *op. cit.* (n. 223), p. 110, citing *RIC Hadrian* 577 and 613, which he knew from H. Cohen, *Description historique des monnaies* Vol. 2 (Paris 1882), p. 121, no. 197 and p. 158, no. 592-3.

[225] H. Mattingly, "Some historical coins of Hadrian", *Journal of Roman Studies* Vol. 15 (1925), pp. 209-222, at p. 214, suggesting that the *Britannia* coin "certainly celebrates the restoration of peace in the North after the revolt under Trajan, in which the Ninth Legion was destroyed", and p. 217, claiming that "Hadrian's departure from

On the whole, the Hadrianic *expeditio Britannica* ("British expedition") had excited little curiosity amongst Mommsen's contemporaries. The great man himself had not even mentioned it, although he surely knew of its existence, if only from the pages of Bruce.[226]

The event was chiefly known from the inscriptions on two statue bases, one long known from Camerinum (present-day Camerino, not far from Ancona), the other discovered in 1850 at Ferentinum (present-day Ferentino, near Rome). Both texts commemorated men who had enjoyed illustrious careers under Hadrian. The first was Marcus Maenius Agrippa, who, having begun his *militia equestris* as prefect of a part-mounted cohort, was *electus a divo Hadriano et missus in expeditionem Britannicam* ("chosen by the deified Hadrian and sent on the British expedition").[227] The second man was Titus Pontius Sabinus, who had abandoned the *militia equestris* after two posts in favour of the centurionate, and having risen rapidly to become *primus pilus* of the Third Augusta Legion, was then assigned as *praepositus vexillationibus milliariis tribus expeditione Brittannica* ("commander of three thousand-strong detachments on the British expedition").[228]

Rome is usually placed in AD 121 and the coins strongly support this dating".

[226] Bruce, *op. cit.* (n. 183), 13, where it was dated to AD 119.

[227] *CIL* XI, 5632 = *ILS* 2735; already known to earlier generations from Orelli, *op. cit.* (n. 4), Vol. 1, p. 193, no. 804.

[228] *CIL* X, 5829 = *ILS* 2726. Published by A. Giorgi, "Iscrizione Ferentinate", *Bullettino dell'Instituto di Corrispondenza Archeologica 1851* (1851), pp. 135-144, incorporating advice sent to him by

Despite the universal recognition that Hadrian himself had visited the province in AD 122, an occasion that surely laid the best claim to the title of *expeditio Britannica*, Weber dated Sabinus' special command to AD 119 (he seems not to have known of Agrippa's involvement), linking it (in a chapter written some years later for the prestigious *Cambridge Ancient History*) with "the crushing of the rebellious Britons, who had destroyed the legion IX Hispana in the camp of Eburacum".[229] Henderson, too (though independently of Weber, whose work he seems not to have consulted), believed that the *expeditio Britannica* had occurred prior to Hadrian's visit.[230]

It is unsurprising that, when Haverfield's student R.G. Collingwood set pen to paper in 1922, he described a similar scenario:[231]

> [Agricola's forts] lasted till late in the reign of Trajan – about 115 – when a great rebellion broke out in Scotland and the north of England. Agricola's forts were swamped one by one, and the Ninth legion, moving up from York to face the insurgents, disappears from history, to be replaced under Hadrian by the 'Victorious' Sixth.

Borghesi earlier that year (*cf. Oeuvres complètes de Bartolomeo Borghesi* Vol. 8, *Lettres* 3 (Paris 1872), pp. 282-288), it was added by Henzen to Orelli, *op. cit.* (n. 4), Vol. 3, p. 84, no. 5456.

[229] W. Weber, "Hadrian", *The Cambridge Ancient History* Vol. 11 (Cambridge 1936) pp. 294-315, at p. 313.

[230] Henderson, *op. cit.* (n. 222), p. 81 and n.8, citing *CIL* X, 5829.

[231] R.G. Collingwood, *Roman Britain* (London 1923), p. 25.

The only element of Mommsen's (and Weber's) story that seemed far-fetched to Collingwood the archaeologist was the destruction of the fortress at Eburacum: "our authorities do not suggest, neither is it reasonable to assume, that the legion was attacked and overwhelmed in its own stronghold".[232] But the rest seemed reasonable. Clearly, it would require a strong intellect to break free of Mommsen's influence and take a measured view of the evidence.

In the 1920s, there was one whose avowed *modus operandi*, "to collect together everything that has been handed down or that can be conjectured" (as stated in his doctoral thesis),[233] held out the hope of producing such an impartial assessment. This was the archaeologist Emil Ritterling, who had recently retired from the post of Museum Director in Wiesbaden due to ill health. Prior to Mommsen's death in 1903, he had been given the great man's blessing to compile an "Index of military matters" for the *Corpus Inscriptionum Latinarum* project, and although such an index never came to fruition, it is quite likely that, when Ritterling was asked to update Grotefend's entry on the Roman legions for the new edition of Pauly's encyclopedia, he had already compiled the basic working data.

The "New Edition" of the *Real-Encyclopädie* had been conceived on a grander scale than the original. Instead of six volumes, the new editor, Georg Wissowa, envisaged ten; but by

---

[232] R.G. Collingwood, "The Roman frontier in Britain", *Antiquity* Vol. 1 (1927), pp. 15-30, at p. 19.

[233] E. Ritterling, *De legione Romanorum X gemina* (Leipzig 1885), p. 1.

1922, eleven volumes had already appeared, each divided into two fascicules, along with three supplementary volumes, sweeping up any subjects that had been missed, and all of this without yet reaching the letter L.

When Ritterling's article duly appeared in Volume 12, like a microcosm of the "New Edition" it dwarfed Grotefend's original in every way. Besides occupying a quarter of the entire volume (it runs to 619 of the 2,552 columns of type), it comprised not only a "History of individual Roman legions in the imperial period" (which had been the basis of Grotefend's article) but also a lengthy preamble discussing the "Registry, distribution, and military activity of the legions", reign by reign, from Augustus to Diocletian. Every statement was backed up with primary evidence or by reference to recent research works.

Of course, it was Ritterling's purpose to elucidate the activities of the legions, not to rewrite the military history of the Roman empire. So, for historical background, he naturally deferred to the handbooks of the day. Consequently, when he stated that the transfer of the Sixth Victrix Legion to Britain was occasioned by a dangerous uprising in AD 119, he cited Weber as his authority.[234] Nevertheless, he speculated that the disappearance of the Ninth Legion may have occurred as late as AD 125, and the earlier transfer of the Sixth Victrix Legion

---

[234] E. Ritterling, "Legio", *Paulys Realencyclopädie der classischen Altertumswissenschaft* Vol. 12, Part 1 (Stuttgart 1924), cols. 1211-1328, at col. 1289, duly noting both *CIL* X, 5829 and XI, 5632.

could have been intended to bolster the provincial army in the face of a major threat.²³⁵

His thinking in this regard was prompted by the nagging doubt that Weber's chronology might not accommodate the careers of those senators who were known to have held a tribunate in the legion. While conceding that Burbuleius Ligarianus might have been tribune in Trajan's later years, he felt that Aemilius Karus' career must have been unduly retarded for his tribunate to have occurred before AD 120, and he wondered whether it was reasonable for Novius Crispinus to have held the consulship fully 30 years after his tribunate, when his peers might expect an interval of only 20 years. Yet who would dare to contradict Mommsen's version of events, backed up by Weber's dating of AD 119? In the end, Ritterling could only suggest that there might have been a second uprising in the mid- or late-120s.²³⁶ The alternative explanation, that the Ninth Legion hadn't after all disappeared in the events of the *expeditio Britannica*, but had continued in existence beyond the 120s, would have been a step too far.

Ritterling appended a list of the Ninth Legion's known officers, amongst whom four familiar names appeared.²³⁷ Sextius Florentinus, who was *legatus legionis* "certainly in the last

---

²³⁵ Ritterling, *op. cit.* (n. 234), col. 1290; *cf.* Ritterling, *op. cit.* (n. 236), col. 1606, questioning whether the Sixth Legion was intended, from the outset, to replace the Ninth.

²³⁶ E. Ritterling, "Legio", *Paulys Realencyclopädie der classischen Altertumswissenschaft* Vol. 12, Part 2 (Stuttgart 1925), cols. 1329-1829, at cols. 1668-1669.

²³⁷ Ritterling, *op. cit.* (n. 236), col. 1669.

years of Trajan or the first of Hadrian"; Aemilius Karus, who was *tribunus militum* "in the first years of Hadrian"; Burbuleius Ligarianus, "at the end of Trajan's reign or the beginning of Hadrian's"; and Novius Crispinus, whose tribunate "could not justifiably have fallen before AD 123". As we have seen, Ritterling could reasonably have pushed that date to AD 128.[238] However, there was another name on the list – Quintus Camurius Numisius Iunior, a man about whom little was yet known to researchers in the 1920s beyond the fact that he had been a tribune,[239] but who would prove to be of great interest in the history of the Ninth Legion.

---

[238] See *supra*, pp. 79-80.
[239] Klebs, *op. cit.* (n. 118), p. 297f., no. C316.

10 AN UNNECESSARY WAR

R ITTERLING'S SUGGESTION of a second British war, born as it was from a desperate attempt to reconcile the prosopographical evidence with the scholarly consensus regarding the fate of the Ninth Legion, found few supporters. Collingwood flatly disagreed. Recounting what is most conveniently termed Mommsen's version of events (though, as we have seen, it was Weber who hammered home the dating), he mentioned, in a footnote, that "Ritterling argues that certain recorded careers suggest a decidedly later date – after 120, and preferably after 125 [but] I cannot think that this is consistent with the legion's absence from the British mural inscriptions".[240]

Some years later, when he came to write the Roman section of *Roman Britain and the English Settlements* for the "Oxford History of England" series, Collingwood explained more fully that "Ritterling asks whether the annihilation of the

---

[240] Collingwood, *op. cit.* (n. 232), p. 19 n. 3.

legion might not have happened in a revolt at some later date in Hadrian's reign", to which he responded: "To my mind, its absence from the inscriptions of the Wall, plus the fact that Hadrian brought the Sixth to Britain (surely to replace it), makes that impossible". And as for Ritterling's observation that "certain persons are known to us who served as tribunes in the Ninth and thereafter passed through other stages in the senatorial career at a rate which, if that legion really ceased to exist in 117-19, was extraordinarily slow", his solution seems with hindsight nothing more than an audacious display of special pleading:[241]

> In any case, the existence of these survivors is proof that the disappearance of the legion was not due to literal annihilation in the field. But a legion that had only suffered severe losses in action was normally brought up to strength by drafts from elsewhere; the suspicion arises, therefore, that the Ninth had not only been cut up, but had disgraced itself, which would account for its survivors' slow promotion.

Of course, this was an example of Collingwood's brand of "constructive history ... interpolating, between the statements borrowed from our authorities, other statements implied by them".[242] He was at pains to emphasize that such interpolation should be "in no way arbitrary or merely fanci-

---

[241] R.G. Collingwood & J.N.L. Myres, *Roman Britain and the English Settlements* (Oxford 1936), pp. 129-130 n. 2.

[242] R.G. Collingwood, *The Idea of History* (Oxford 1946) p. 240.

ful". Yet on this occasion, he had failed his own test of subjecting a hypothesis to critical thinking; otherwise, he might have paused to reflect on how his proposed branding of at least two future consuls as disgraced survivors might seem, in the absence of any supporting evidence, to be both arbitrary and fanciful.

Nevertheless, his scenario was enthusiastically adopted, though without attribution, by his pupil and colleague Ian Richmond. All the more ironic, given Richmond's criticism of *Roman Britain and the English Settlements*, that "there are many points in which his text goes far beyond the evidence".[243] For, having arrived at the relevant point in his own *Roman Britain* book, he boldly informed his readers (without acknowledging his source):[244]

> Certain it is that immediately after Trajan's death in AD 117 trouble came which involved heavy Roman casualties and which Fronto, writing two generations later, remembered as especially notable. This is to be connected with the fact that by AD 122 the Ninth Legion was replaced at York by the Sixth and disappeared from the army lists thereafter. That the Legion was cashiered there is no doubt and it seems evident

---

[243] I.A. Richmond, "Appreciation of R.G. Collingwood as an archaeologist", *Proceedings of the British Academy* Vol. 29 (1944), pp. 476-480, at p. 478.

[244] I.A. Richmond, *Roman Britain* (Harmondsworth 1955), p. 47. The absence of *Roman Britain and the English Settlements* from Richmond's bibliography (pp. 215-217) is puzzling.

that this fate, at the hands of the disciplinarian Hadrian, followed an ignominious defeat. But the unit was not annihilated. Some of its officers at least survived and nothing whatever is reported of the circumstances or place of the trouble. The steps which Hadrian took to repair the damage suggest, however, that the seat of disturbance lay in south-western Scotland.

It is more than a little peculiar that Richmond chose not to mention the alternative solution proposed by his Durham colleague Eric Birley, whose archaeological expertise was matched only by his prosopographical knowledge. Birley firmly believed that "the careers to which we have referred do not permit us to accept the traditional view of a disaster to *IX Hispana* in the early years of Hadrian".[245]

Birley's solution was to concur with Ritterling and posit a second period of serious warfare in Britain, later in Hadrian's reign. He was intrigued by the fact that Sextus Julius Severus, a man whom the historian Cassius Dio called "foremost amongst Hadrian's best generals",[246] had been governing the province when the emperor withdrew him to take command in the Jewish War of AD 132-136, an event of such magnitude that it cast a shadow over Hadrian's final years. The departure

---

[245] E. Birley, "Britain after Agricola, and the end of the Ninth Legion", *Roman Britain and the Roman Army. Collected Papers* (Kendal 1953), pp. 20-30, at p. 27, reprinted from the *Durham University Journal* (June 1948), pp. 78-83.

[246] Dio, *Roman History* 69.13.2.

of Severus, he reasoned, no doubt accompanied by troops destined for the eastern theatre, might well have provoked the Britons to further hostilities. On the other hand, the presence of such a man as governor in the first place might suggest that trouble had already broken out. Either way, he believed that "*IX Hispana*'s end may have come in or about 130".[247]

It is worth remembering that even Collingwood himself had realized that "the only reason for imagining a disaster of any magnitude is the unexplained disappearance of the Ninth legion".[248] Hadrian's reign had certainly opened with warfare, but the known facts were few and fairly straightforward, as another Hadrian's Wall scholar, J.P. Gillam, stated with great clarity:[249]

> On the accession of the Emperor Hadrian, Britain, we are told, was restive; elsewhere we learn that in his reign many Roman soldiers lost their lives in Britain. The details of the trouble at this time are obscure; … It is not known whether there was a revolt, or whether the province, whose boundary may have lain at this time either roughly on the line of the present Border, or already on the Tyne-Solway isthmus, was invaded from without.

---

[247] Birley, *op. cit.* (n. 245), p. 28.

[248] Collingwood, *op. cit.* (n. 241), p. 128.

[249] J.P. Gillam, "Roman and native, AD 122-197", in I.A. Richmond (ed.), *Roman and Native in North Britain* (Edinburgh 1958), pp. 60-90, at p. 60. See *supra*, nn. 110-111 for the sources.

The emperor himself had visited the province, as he had visited many others, and two officers (Marcus Maenius Agrippa and Titus Pontius Sabinus) were known to have taken part in an *expeditio Britannica*. It was this latter event, normally assumed to have been Hadrian's visit in AD 122, that Birley now proposed redating to AD 130, though he did not specify his "strong chronological reasons".[250]

In the end, it was left to Birley's student Michael Jarrett, some years later, to examine anew the careers of the two officers in question. He concluded that there were, in fact, no strong chronological reasons to postpone the *expeditio Britannica*, as the careers of the two men could comfortably accommodate the accepted date of AD 122.[251] Another of Birley's students, Brian Dobson, having subjected the career of one of the men, Sabinus, to particular scrutiny, arrived at the same conclusion.[252]

In the meantime, Richmond continued to repeat the version of events that he had appropriated from Collingwood; namely, that "the conditions are adequate to cover a disgraceful defeat of the Ninth, meriting at the hands of the disciplinarian Hadrian the cashiering of the unit".[253] He even took pains to underline Weber's favoured dating, when he added

---

[250] Birley, *loc. cit.* (n. 247).

[251] M.G. Jarrett, "An unnecessary war", *Britannia* Vol. 7 (1976), pp. 145-151.

[252] B. Dobson, *Die Primipilares* (Köln 1978), pp. 235-236, no. 117.

[253] I.A. Richmond, "Introduction", *An Inventory of the historical monuments in the City of York. Vol 1. Eburacum: Roman York* (London 1962), pp. xxix-xli, at p. xxxii.

– in one of the minor revisions for the second edition of his *Roman Britain* – that the event "is to be connected with the issue of victory coins in AD 119".[254] And it was surely in particular response to Birley's theory that he added: "The later the event is placed the more difficult it is to account for, and no strain is involved in associating the disbanding of the unit, whose staff officers at least survived, with the visit of Hadrian to Britain in AD 121–2".[255]

On the contrary, we can be fairly certain that the Ninth Legion was not disbanded in disgrace, for this would surely have entailed *damnatio memoriae*, whereas its name survived unscathed on so many inscriptions, unlike that of the Third Augusta Legion, which was neatly chiselled from any inscriptions erected prior to its temporary disbanding in AD 238.[256] Nevertheless, eccentric as the notion of disgrace and disbanding might be, there was evidently still scope to develop it further, with the unlikely suggestion that "the Ninth was the victim of mass desertions from 119 onwards, and that it dwindled away until the authorities decided to disband it altogether".[257]

Here matters might have remained, with two camps effectively at loggerheads, both trying to squeeze the evidence into

---

[254] I.A. Richmond, *Roman Britain* (2nd edn. Harmondsworth 1963), p. 47.

[255] Richmond, *loc. cit.* (n. 253).

[256] Ritterling, *op. cit.* (n. 236), cols. 1336 and 1501.

[257] T. Stanier, "The Brigantes and the Ninth Legion", *Phoenix* Vol. 19 (1965), pp. 305-313, at p. 311, surely influenced by *The Eagle of the Ninth*.

the straitjacket that Mommsen's *Provinzen* had forced on them. Unwisely taking their cue from a doctoral thesis by a man of whom it was said that his "choice of facts, in point of relevance or veracity, is not always of the happiest",[258] a succession of British archaeologists believed, as an absolute and incontrovertible truth, that the Ninth Legion had met its end in Britain prior to AD 120, while only Ritterling and Birley, following Borghesi's prosopographical approach, realized that the known facts about men serving in that legion would not allow it.

---

[258] R. Syme, review of W. Weber's *Rom, Herrschertum und Reich im zweiten Jahrhundert* (1937), in *The Classical Review* Vol. 53 (1939), pp. 79-80, at p. 80. The book was an expanded version of Weber's contributions to *The Cambridge Ancient History* Vol. 11 (see *supra*, n. 229).

11 TAKING THE WATERS

Prior to the 1960s, no one would have entertained the thought that the fate of the Ninth Legion might lie elsewhere than in Britain. But a flurry of continental evidence was about to take the debate in another direction.

For many, their first inkling would have come in 1967, upon opening the pages of a new history of Roman Britain from the pen of Sheppard Frere, Professor of the Archaeology of the Roman Empire at Oxford. Frere wrote that "there are grounds for doubting whether Legio IX was lost as early as 117-118".[259]

It is worth noting, in passing, that he had tacitly revised Weber's date of AD 119 for the crushing of the supposed insurrection by reference to the speculative reconstruction of two fragments from a damaged inscription, which he took to refer to a victory in the year of Hadrian's second consulship

---

[259] S.S. Frere, *Britannia. A history of Roman Britain* (London 1967), p. 138.

(AD 118).[260] However, the reading of the critical line has always been controversial, for, although the drawing prepared by the inscription's editors shows COS II (as duly reported in the version published in *L'année épigraphique*), the editors themselves clearly preferred to read *[-- c]o(n)s(ul) II[I --]*, in order to date the inscription to AD 119.[261]

As for the loss of the legion, Frere had been persuaded by Birley's interpretation of the *expeditio Britannica* into believing that "the scattered threads of evidence all suggest serious fighting in Britain about 130, and this would suit the appointment of Julius Severus to the British command about that year, since he was one of the foremost generals of the day".[262]

Readers would have been forgiven for assuming that Frere was arguing in favour of the destruction of the Ninth Legion around AD 130, particularly as, in his discussion of the Antonine advance into Scotland a few pages later, he suggested that "it may even be that the annihilation of Legio IX was a

---

[260] Frere, *op. cit.* (n. 259), p. 126, alluding to *RIB* 1051.

[261] I.A. Richmond & R.P. Wright, "Stones from a Hadrianic war memorial on Tyneside", *Archaeologia Aeliana*[4] Vol. 21 (1943), pp. 93-120, whence *AE* 1947, 123. Hübner, *op. cit.* (n. 42), p. 108, no. 498, was unable to decipher the line in question. R.S.O. Tomlin, "Addenda and corrigenda", in R.G. Collingwood & R.P. Wright, *The Roman Inscriptions of Britain* (2nd edn. Stroud 1995), pp. 751-800, at p. 778, regards the interpretation of Richmond and Wright as "far from certain" on account of the damage to the inscription.

[262] Frere, *op. cit.* (n. 259), p. 139.

determining factor".[263] But in the midst of this, almost as an afterthought, he inserted the following passage:[264]

> But there remains also the probability that the legion was withdrawn from Britain at some date between 108 and 122 and that it perished unrecorded later on, either in Judaea in 132-135 or later still. Evidence which might support such a view is the discovery of a tile-stamp and a mortarium-stamp of Legio IX at Nijmegen in Holland. ... These finds certainly suggest that the Ninth may have been stationed at Nijmegen for a short time at some period after 108, the latest date known for its presence at York, and perhaps from about 121. Further evidence is needed before more can be said.

Frere's book was greeted warmly by an array of distinguished reviewers, only one of whom appears to have noticed the rather disconnected text. This was Denis Henry, the Assistant Master at Stonyhurst College, Lancashire, who nevertheless did not quibble that the author seemed to be eating his cake and having it by presenting two contrasting probabilities, but simply noted that, regarding the legion's disappearance, Frere "does not regard a definite conclusion as possible yet in the present state of evidence".[265]

---

[263] Frere, *op. cit.* (n. 259), p. 150.

[264] Frere, *op. cit.* (n. 259), pp. 139-140.

[265] D. Henry, Review of Frere (*op. cit.*, n. 259), *Classical Philology* Vol. 64 (1969), pp. 243-247, at p. 244.

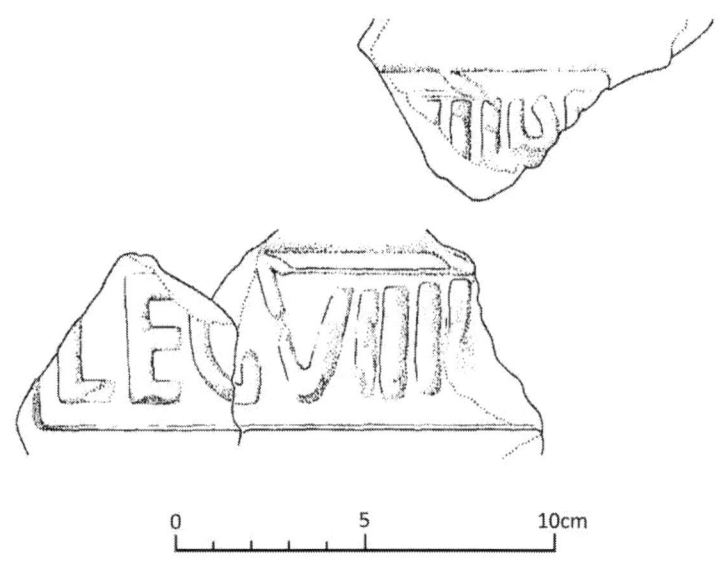

Figure 12: Two fragments of tile from Nijmegen

The evidence from the Netherlands, alluded to by Frere, albeit rather mysteriously,[266] had been publicly announced in 1964, at the Sixth International "Limeskongress" (the forum for Roman frontier studies), although Dutch archaeologists and their correspondents had been aware of it for somewhat longer.[267] Limeskongress participants were shown a fragment of a *tegula* that had been excavated in 1959 from the final

---

[266] His source was, in fact, cited some pages earlier, on p. 123 n. 2, in connection with the "auxiliary vexillation" of *ILS* 2515 returning to Britain from Pannonia, where Frere mentions Bogaers' contribution to the 1964 Limeskongress (see *infra*, n. 268).

[267] The epigrapher R.P. Wright alludes to a letter from J.E. Bogaers on the subject, dated 28 July 1962, in "Tile-Stamps of the Ninth Legion found in Britain", *Britannia* 9 (1978), pp. 379-382, at p. 381 n. 9.

occupation layer of an area of barrack blocks inside the legionary fortress at Noviodunum (present-day Nijmegen). It was stamped LEG VIIII (fig. 12).[268]

During the later 1950s and 1960s, excavations on the Hunerberg at Nijmegen had revealed a large area of the 16ha fortress known to have been occupied by the Tenth Gemina Legion. Archaeology suggested that the legion had begun building a timber fortress in AD 70, following the crushing of the Batavian Revolt, but that, within a generation, refurbishing in stone commenced. Such construction work was common during Trajan's reign and men from the three legions of Germania Inferior (the First Minervia, Sixth Victrix, and Tenth Gemina Legions) were known to be quarrying building stone at Brohltal in AD 101-102.[269] But within a year or two, the troop build-up for Trajan's Second Dacian War had drawn away the First Minervia Legion, soon followed by the Tenth Gemina Legion. Neither was destined to return.

Dutch archaeologists believed that the Hunerberg fortress was occupied thereafter by a composite garrison of troops

---

[268] J.E. Bogaers, "Die Besatzungstruppen des Legionslagers von Nijmegen im 2. Jahrhundert nach Christus", *Studien zu den Militärgrenzen Roms. Vorträge des 6. internationalen Limeskongresses in Süddeutschland* (Cologne 1967), pp. 54-76, at pp. 63-64 and 68-72, with Tafel 5, no. 3. A second example was discovered in 1966: J.E. Bogaers & J.K. Haalebos, "Die Nijmegener Legionslager seit 70 nach Christus", *Studien zu den Militärgrenzen Roms II. Vorträge des 10. Internationalen Limeskongresses in der Germania Inferior* (Cologne 1977), pp. 93-108, at p. 107.

[269] *CIL* XIII, 7697, 7715, 7716.

drawn from Britain. Over 100 tiles stamped *VEX(illatio) BRIT-(annica)* were recovered from the site, as well as from the nearby tile-works at De Holdeurn.[270] Finds from this final phase of the fortress were sparse but included early second-century pottery and coins of Trajan and Hadrian, while the neighbouring *canabae legionis* (the civil settlement closely associated with the fortress) remained occupied until the middle of the 2nd century.[271] However, it was chiefly the presence of tiles of the Thirtieth Ulpia Victrix Legion, though in considerably lesser numbers, that led archaeologists to date the final phase of refurbishment in the fortress to the period after AD 120, as this legion was thought to have arrived in Lower Germany in that year. This was the context into which the Ninth Legion tiles fitted.[272]

The Dutch archaeologist Jules Bogaers observed that, on the numerous stamped tiles of the Ninth Legion known from York, the legion's numeral took the form "IX", whereas on the Nijmegen tile-stamps, the numeral had been rendered as "VIIII". However, this same form of the numeral occurred on

---

[270] *CIL* XIII, 12553. H. Brunsting & D.C. Steures, "De baksteenstempels van Romeins Nijmegen 1. Opgravingen castra 1950-1967, Opgravingen Kops Plateau, ca. 1986-1994", *Oudheidkundige Mededelingen uit het Rijksmuseum van Oudheden te Leiden* 75 (1995), pp. 85-117, at pp. 104-107.

[271] *E.g.* J.K. Haalebos, *Castra und Canabae. Ausgrabungen auf dem Hunerberg in Nijmegen 1987-1994* (Nijmegen 1995), p. 86.

[272] *E.g.* J.K. Haalebos, "Romeinse troepen in Nijmegen", *Bijdragen en Mededelingen* 91 (2000), pp. 9-36.

tile-stamps of the legion from the tile-works at Scalesceugh in Cumbria, and at the nearby forts of Carlisle and Stanwix.[273]

Sadly, the Scalesceugh tile-works have never been properly investigated so no chronology has ever been established. But the archaeologist Brian Hartley noted a drop in the quantities of samian pottery found at York, and suggested that, from around AD 110, much of the legion's manpower had been absent on a building project, perhaps even the construction of a new fortress, in the Carlisle area.[274] Bogaers suggested that it was from there that the legion decamped to the Continent, bringing the distinctive stamp used at Scalesceugh with them. He fixed its arrival at Nijmegen around AD 121, as a respite from the fighting in Britain at the outset of Hadrian's reign.[275]

One other item was unveiled at the 1964 Limeskongress, an item that had only come to light two years earlier, despite having been discovered during the first excavations at the De Holdeurn tile-works in 1938. This was part of the rim of a type of coarseware ceramic mixing bowl known as a mortarium. Along its top edge, the stamp of the Ninth Legion could clearly be seen: *L(e)G VIIII HIS(pana)*.[276] No similar item was

---

[273] Wright, *op. cit.* (n. 267), whence *RIB* 2462. Hübner, *op. cit.* (n. 42), p. 226, knew only the "IX" tile-stamps. The "VIIII" examples only came to light from the 1890s onwards.

[274] B.R. Hartley, "Roman York and the northern military command to the third century AD", in R.M. Butler (ed.), *Soldier and Civilian in Roman Yorkshire* (Leicester 1971), pp. 55-69, at p. 60.

[275] Bogaers, *op. cit.* (n. 268), p. 74.

[276] Bogaers, *op. cit.* (n. 268), pp. 63-64 and 71, with Tafel 5, no. 4.

known from Britain, where the Roman army did not appear to have manufactured its own mortaria, requisitioning them instead from the civilian potters of the south. Clearly, a different tradition obtained on the Continent, and any legion installed at Nijmegen was obliged to manufacture its own coarseware pottery.

Bogaers summarised the significance of this new evidence for the benefit of Limeskongress delegates:

> However small the traces of legio IX Hispana may be in the Netherlands so far, from the available data it must probably be concluded that the entire legion had lain briefly in the fortress at Nijmegen and that soldiers of this legion were working in the brickworks and potteries at De Holduern.

But these were not the only traces of the Ninth Legion in the province of Germania Inferior. Some years earlier, in 1957, an altar to Apollo had been discovered during excavations at Aquae Granni (present-day Aachen-Burtscheid in northern Germany). It had been set up by Lucius Latinius Macer from Verona, who described himself as *p(rimus)p(ilus) leg(ionis) IX Hisp(anae) praef(ectus) castr(orum)* ("chief centurion of the Ninth Hispana Legion, prefect of the camp").[277]

---

[277] H. Nesselhauf & H. von Petrikovits, "Ein Weihaltar für Apollo aus Aachen-Burtscheid", *Bonner Jahrbücher* Vol. 167 (1967), pp. 268-279, whence *AE* 1968, 323. The find was first mentioned by J.E. Bogaers, "Romeins Nijmegen. De bezettingstroepen van de Nijmeegse Legioensvesting in de 2de eeuw na Chr.", *Numaga* 12 (1965), pp. 10-37, at pp. 29-30.

The find-spot at the hot springs of Aachen, and the deity, Apollo Grannus, depicted in relief on the front face of the altar holding his characteristic lyre, suggest that Macer had come to seek healing, and the fact that he *v(otum) s(olvit) l(ibens) m(erito)* ("gladly and deservedly fulfilled his vow") shows that he found it.

Macer had been promoted to the position of *praefectus castrorum* from *primus pilus*, the crucial role that guaranteed entry to the ranks of the elite *primipilares*. This led Herbert Nesselhauf, in his discussion of the inscription, to postulate that he had risen through the centurionate, comparing him to another *primus pilus* of the Ninth Legion, Marcus Cocceius Severus, whose memorial Mommsen had seen in Turin Museum.[278]

In fact, Birley had already drawn attention to the possibility that Severus had served in the Ninth Legion much later than its presumed Hadrianic demise.[279] Arguing from the supposition that he had received his citizenship on enlistment from the emperor Marcus Cocceius Nerva, from whom he would have taken his distinctive name, Birley suggested that he had slowly risen through the centurionate under Trajan and Hadrian, arriving at the post of *primus pilus* in the Ninth Legion early in the reign of Antoninus Pius, at the age of around 60. Dobson, on the other hand, thought it more likely that Severus had come from long-established citizen stock in

---

[278] Th. Mommsen, *Corpus Inscriptionum Latinarum* Vol. 5: *Inscriptiones Galliae Cisalpinae Latinae*, Part 2 (Berlin 1877), p. 803, no. 7159.

[279] Birley, *op. cit.* (n. 245), pp. 26-27.

north Italy, where Cocceius was a reasonably common name, and might already have reached the primipilate under Trajan.[280]

Likewise, there is no reason to postulate a lengthy career for Macer, whose Italian origin suggested to Dobson that he had probably been a Praetorian, who took the fast track into the legionary centurionate.[281] However, the inscription's real importance, as Nesselhauf noted, lay in the fact that, if a legion's *praefectus castrorum* was present, the legion could not be far away,[282] for no officer of this rank would be in charge of a detachment.[283] Here was further proof that the Ninth Legion had taken up residence at Nijmegen.

Nesselhauf saw no reason to keep the Ninth Legion in Britain much beyond AD 108, the date of its construction work at York, and every reason to date its occupation at Nijmegen as early as possible. He was exercised by Hadrian's decision to transfer the Sixth Victrix Legion from Lower Germany to Britain (which he incidentally redated to AD 119), for he believed that, if the Ninth Legion had been at Nijmegen, it would have been the natural choice to return to a familiar theatre of operations. Thus, according to Nesselhauf's theory, by AD 119, the Ninth Legion had already moved on. He found a plausible explanation in the troop movements for Trajan's Parthian

---

[280] Dobson, *op. cit.* (n. 252), p.260, no. 141.

[281] Dobson, *op. cit.* (n. 252), pp. 233-4, no. 114.

[282] Nesselhauf & Petrikovits, *op. cit.* (n. 277), pp. 270-271.

[283] *Contra* Haalebos, *op. cit.* (n. 272), p. 22. Dando-Collins, *op. cit.* (n. 320), p. 424, commits the same error.

War, which saw entire legions shuffled along the Danube in a process that is still only imperfectly understood, and suggested that the legion arrived in the East "in the extremely critical situation created by the unfavourable outcome of the Parthian War and the revolt of the Jews, which spread rapidly in a hinterland that was no longer sufficiently protected".[284]

Bogaers had also argued that, at some stage, the Ninth Legion ended up on the eastern frontier. This was based on the evidence of an undated tombstone from Naples, commemorating a *mil(es) leg(ionis) IX* ("soldier of the Ninth Legion") named Aelius Asclepiades, *natione Cilix* ("a Cilician by birth").[285] Bogaers took the man's name as proof that he had enlisted during the reign of Hadrian, as it was common for non-citizen recruits to adopt the emperor's family name (in this case, Aelius), and he cited the man's nationality (from Cilicia, in the south-east of present-day Turkey) as proof that he had joined the legion in the East. A likely context for this, and for the legion's demise, was therefore presented by Hadrian's Jewish War of AD 132-136.

In fact, Aelius Asclepiades had already been noticed by the archaeologist John Mann, who commented that "it is difficult to see how this man of eastern origin could have reached IX Hispana, unless the legion had been moved from Britain to the east, or how a man with the *nomen* Aelius could have been

---

[284] Nesselhauf & Petrikovits, *op. cit.* (n. 277), p. 273.
[285] Bogaers, *op. cit.* (n. 277), p. 25; *idem, op. cit.* (n. 268), p. 73, citing *CIL* X, 1769.

recruited to it, unless it had survived for some time into the reign of Hadrian".[286]

The alternative suggestion, made by A.R. Birley,[287] that the man had transferred to the legion from the Roman imperial fleet at Misenum (present-day Miseno, near Naples), where other Cilician marines are known,[288] permitted the archaeologist Lawrence Keppie to question the dating. Observing that, "if he had been recently given citizenship by Hadrian, the form P. Aelius Aclepiades might have been expected", Keppie suggested that his name "may have no chronological implications for his later service".[289]

The inscription, known only from the written record of the eighteenth-century Naples antiquarian Alessio Mazzocchi,[290]

---

[286] J.C. Mann, *The Settlement of Veterans in the Roman Empire* (unpublished PhD thesis, London 1956) p. 274-5 n. 11, published as *Legionary Recruitment and Veteran Settlement during the Principate* (London 1983), p. 177 n. 473.

[287] A.R. Birley, *The Fasti of Roman Britain* (Oxford 1981), p. 222 n. 27; *idem*, *The Roman Government of Britain* (Oxford 2005), p. 229 n. 20.

[288] *CIL* VI, 3113, 3123, 3129; X, 3372, 3377, 3402, 3424, 3443, 3445, 3454, 3558, 3604, 3605, 3623, 3651, 3662; XIV, 3627; *AE* 1972, 80. The nameless Cilician marine on *CIL* X, 3668 probably belonged to the Misene fleet as well, while the Cilician on *CIL* XI, 110 must have belonged to the Ravenna fleet.

[289] L. Keppie, "The fate of the Ninth Legion. A problem for the eastern provinces?" in D.H. French & C.S. Lightfoot (eds.), *The Eastern Frontier of the Roman Empire* (Oxford 1989), pp. 247-255, at p. 251.

[290] A. Gervasio, "Osservazioni intorno alcune antiche iscrizioni che sono o furono già in Napoli", *Memorie della regale Accademia Ercolanese di archeologia* Vol. 5 (1846), pp.81-155, at p. 133 no. 3, whence *CIL* X, 1769.

has long been lost, so the text cannot be subjected to renewed scrutiny, but it must be admitted that it would be unusual for the Ninth Legion to appear without its epithet on a second-century inscription. Nevertheless, if the case for a transfer from the fleet is accepted, we must look for a suitable emergency, the most obvious being Hadrian's Jewish War, in connection with which other marines from Misenum are known to have been drafted into the Tenth Fretensis Legion.[291] But, as Keppie reminds us, "the inscription itself, which is not closely datable, gives no hint of such a transfer".[292]

The evidence from Nijmegen had certainly opened up exciting new possibilities for the fate of the Ninth Legion. It only remained to see whether the academic world would adopt Bogaers' theory or Nesselhauf's theory, or neither.

---

[291] As noted by Birley, *locc. citt.* (n. 287), citing *CIL* XVI, app. 13 (= *PSI* IX, 1026).

[292] Keppie, *loc. cit.* (n. 289).

12 THE CONSUL OF AD 161

FRUSTRATINGLY, THE EVIDENCE of the Ninth Legion in Germania Inferior could not be slotted neatly into a particular time-frame, as a number of scholars were quick to point out.[293] Archaeologists Michael Jarrett and John Mann, in a short survey of the military history of the province of Britannia, emphasized that "the evidence indicates that IX Hispana survived into at least the middle years of Hadrian's reign, and we are not justified in supposing that it survived as anything but a full legion".[294] This was clearly a riposte, not only to those who favoured the dwindling away of the legion until only a few staff officers remained, but also to those who postulated a destruction prior to AD 122.

---

[293] A silvered bronze pendant stamped LEG IX HISP, found at Ewijk near Nijmegen, is similarly undated: P.J. Sijpestijn, "Die *legio nona Hispana* in Nimwegen", *Zeitschrift für Papyrologie und Epigraphik* Vol. 111 (1996), pp. 281-282, whence *AE* 1996, 1107.

[294] M.G. Jarrett & J.C. Mann, "Britain from Agricola to Gallienus", *Bonner Jahrbücher* Vol. 170 (1970), pp. 178-210, at p. 184.

As for the legion's sojourn at Nijmegen, Jarrett and Mann considered the most obvious occasion to be during Trajan's Second Dacian War, after which "the men will have returned to York before the stone building there was far advanced".[295] This was even earlier than Nesselhauf was willing to accept; for him, "a temporary posting [to Nijmegen] during the legion's British residence is virtually out of the question".[296]

This was also the considered opinion of Eric Birley, who thought it unlikely that, in the later years of Trajan's reign, Britain would have been downgraded to a two-legion province, and furthermore that it would have been the legion in the north, the scene of previous and subsequent trouble, that was earmarked for withdrawal. But equally, he found Nesselhauf's preferred chronology uncomfortable, with the Sixth Victrix and Ninth Hispana legions moving in opposite directions within the period AD 114-119. Rather, he conjectured that the evidence from Scalesceugh (which Nesselhauf had not addressed) might imply that a Carlisle fortress had been on the cards for the Ninth Legion, until the building of the large Hadrian's Wall cavalry fort at nearby Stanwix removed the need for it, by which time the Sixth Legion was comfortably installed at York and the simplest solution was to transfer the Ninth to the vacant fortress at Nijmegen.[297]

---

[295] Jarret & Mann, *op. cit.* (n. 294), p. 185.

[296] Nesselhauf & Petrikovits, *op. cit.* (n. 277), p. 272.

[297] E. Birley, "The fate of the Ninth Legion", in R.M. Butler (ed.), *Soldier and Civilian in Roman Yorkshire* (Leicester 1971), pp. 71-80, at pp. 75-77.

However, although Jarrett and Mann had explained away the Nijmegen evidence as indicating only a short-term occupation around AD 105, the former remained non-committal about the legion's subsequent movements, while the latter still thought it most likely that it "was transferred to the east for Trajan's Parthian War, remaining in the east to be destroyed in the second Jewish rebellion of AD 132-5".[298]

Birley also countered this suggestion with his own, that the Ninth Legion might even have been the unnamed unit that Cassius Dio claimed to have been destroyed by the Parthians at Elegeia in AD 161.[299] His article prompted a swift reply from the German epigrapher Werner Eck, for a newly published military diploma had provided a date for another of Ritterling's tribunes.[300] This was Quintus Camurius Numisius Iunior.

In fact, Numisius had first come to light in 1845, when the antiquarian Camillo Ramelli wrote an open letter to Wilhelm Henzen, describing some new epigraphic discoveries from the neighbourhood of his native Fabriano near Ancona. Three of the inscriptions mentioned Numisius, whose career Ramelli had managed to tease out, with some assistance from

---

[298] Mann, *loc. cit.* (n. 286, 1983).

[299] Birley, *op. cit.* (n. 297), p. 74. His suggestion was first noted by Bogaers, *op. cit.* (n. 277), p. 30. For Elegeia, see *supra*, p. 34 and n. 65.

[300] B. Overbeck, "Ein neues Militärdiplom von Moesia superior", *Chiron* 2 (1972), pp. 449-458, whence *AE* 1972, 657 = M. Roxan, *Roman Military Diplomas 1954-1977* (London 1978), pp. 78-79, no. 55.

Borghesi.[301] It seems that Numisius had spent his vigintivirate in the prestigious role of mint-master (*triumvir auro argento aere flando feriundo*), before becoming *tr[ib(unus) mil(itum)] leg(ionis) VIIII Hi[sp(anae)]* ("tribune of the Ninth Hispana Legion"). He perhaps enjoyed imperial patronage, since after entry to the senate as *quaestor urbanus* ("urban quaestor", perhaps attached to one of the consuls), he served as *ae[d(ilis) cur(ulis)]* ("curule aedile") rather than tribune of the plebs. He went on to command two legions in succession, a reasonably unusual occurrence perhaps occasioned by some emergency, and although the name of the first one is illegible on the inscription, the second one (being Numisius' most recent post when the inscription was cut) was the Sixth Victrix Legion in Britain.

With such early promise and two children (the inscription appears to have been erected by *[--] et [Iu]nior pa[tri]*, "... and Iunior for their father"), rapid advance to the consulship could be envisaged.

As for the dating of Numisius' career, Borghesi had advised Ramelli that "he must have flourished no later than Antoninus Pius, since after the triumvirate of the mint, he was tribune of the legion VIIII Hispanica, which was lost under

---

[301] C. Ramelli, "Iscrizioni di Fabriano", *Bullettino dell'Instituto di Corrispondenza Archeologica 1845* (1845), pp. 127-137, at pp. 128-129. The three inscriptions were published by E. Bormann, *Corpus Inscriptionum Latinarum* Vol. 11: *Inscriptiones Aemiliae Etruriae Umbriae Latinae*, Part 2, Fasc. 1 (Berlin 1901), p. 826, nos. 5670-5672. Henzen included the first of these, as the most informative, in his supplement to Orelli, *op. cit.* (n. 4), p. 202, no. 6050.

the reign of Hadrian".[302] Consequently, Ritterling had registered his command of the Sixth Victrix Legion as "probably under Trajan or Hadrian",[303] though he hazarded no guess as to the season of his tribunate.

Thus, the information from the new diploma, that Numisius had been consul on 8 February AD 161, came as a welcome surprise, for it allowed Eck to place his tribunate of the Ninth Legion "not before AD 140/141".[304] As the editors of *L'année épigraphique* succinctly noted, "this conclusively demolishes the idea of this legion's disappearance under Hadrian and confirms the thesis of E. Birley, according to which the IX *Hispana* legion was not annihilated in Britain, but took part in an eastern expedition".[305]

Nevertheless, a different (indeed, some might say contrary) view was taken by Keppie, who denied that the tribune of the Ninth Legion was the same man as the consul of AD 161. His portrayal of Numisius' birthplace as an "isolated one-horse town" and his assumption that Numisius' father was not a senator were perhaps intended to cast doubt on the man's suitability for high office, for Keppie preferred to

---

[302] Quoted by Ramelli, *op. cit.* (n. 301), p. 130.

[303] Ritterling, *op. cit.* (n. 236), col. 1610.

[304] W. Eck, "Zum Ende der *legio IX Hispana*", *Chiron* 2 (1972), pp. 459-462, at p. 462. The date of Numisius' consulship is also confirmed by *AE* 1984, 529 = M. Roxan, *Roman Military Diplomas 1978-1984* (London 1985), pp. 178-9, no. 107.

[305] J. Gagé, M. Leglay, H.-G. Pflaum & P. Wuilleumier (eds.), *L'année épigraphique 1972* (Paris 1975), p. 209.

suppose that "the consul of AD 161 was the son or grandson of the tribune".[306]

Naturally, this played to Keppie's belief in "a shorter rather than a longer lifespan for the legion",[307] but required him to gamble upon a man whose very existence is based on the survival of four letters on his father's statue base, in preference to one whose early career showed exactly the kind of promise that would culminate in a consulship. Although the French historian Yann Le Bohec thought Keppie's theory "seductive",[308] most researchers preferred Eck's analysis of Numisius' career.[309]

Meanwhile, historians of Roman Britain scrambled to assimilate the new findings. While Frere, through subsequent editions of *Britannia*, clung stubbornly to his version of events that saw the cashiering of a disgraced legion ("annihilation is unlikely, since the names of several survivors are known") in

---

[306] Keppie, *op. cit.* (n. 289), pp. 251-252; *idem*, "Legiones II Augusta, VI Victrix, IX Hispana, XX Valeria Victrix", in Y. Le Bohec (ed.), *Les légions de Rome sous le Haut-Empire* (Lyon 2000), pp. 25-37, at p. 29 n. 61.

[307] L. Keppie, "Legio VIIII in Britain: the Beginning and the End", in R. Brewer (ed.), *Roman Fortresses and their Legions* (London & Cardiff 2000), pp. 83-100, at p. 94.

[308] Y. Le Bohec, "Remarques historiques sur des inscriptions militaires d'Ombrie", in M. Medri (ed.), *Sentinum 295 a.C. Sassoferrato 2006. 2300 anni dopo la battaglia* (Rome 2008), pp. 31-43, at p. 32.

[309] Enshrined as W. Eck, "Numisius (4a)", *Paulys Realencyclopädie der classischen Altertumswissenschaft* Suppl. 14 (Munich 1974), cols. 287-288. Accepted by (*e.g.*) G. Alföldy, *Konsulat und Senatorenstand unter die Antoninen* (Bonn 1977), p. 171 n. 137, and 336; Birley, *opp. citt.* (n. 287), 1981, pp. 254-256; 2005, pp. 256-257.

the aftermath of an insurrection that ended in AD 118 ("but a date of about 130 would suit the careers of the men involved better than a date of about 118"), all the while retaining the option of his alternative probability,[310] others had taken the new evidence fully into account.

The year 1981 saw the publication of two new histories. In Peter Salway's *Roman Britain*, a massive tome advertised as the replacement for Collingwood's volume in the "Oxford History of Britain" series, the author followed Birley's line of argumentation, with a transfer of "the unlucky Ninth legion" from Carlisle to Nijmegen around AD 126 before being "sent to the east, to disappear in the Jewish wars of the 130s or against the Parthians in 161".[311] Archaeologist Malcolm Todd, on the other hand, in a book hailed by reviewers for its conciseness, at least pointed his readers to Bogaers, Nesselhauf, and Eck, so that they might make up their own minds. His summary of the topic, like the book as a whole, was a model of brevity:[312]

> The problem of when this legion left Britain and what its eventual fate was still baffles reasonable conjecture. ... The warfare at the very end of Trajan's reign, only concluded by a Roman victory in 119, provides a likely occasion, but there could have been others. ...

---

[310] S.S. Frere, *Britannia. A history of Roman Britain* (2nd edn. London 1978), pp. 161-162; (3rd edn. London 1987), pp. 122-124.

[311] P. Salway, *Roman Britain* (Oxford 1981), p. 174.

[312] M. Todd, *Roman Britain 55 BC – AD 400. The Province beyond Ocean* (Glasgow 1981), p. 121.

The continued survival of the unit at least down to the beginning of the reign of Antoninus Pius, however, now seems probable; it may not have met its end until the early years of Marcus Aurelius.

It seems that a new orthodoxy had arrived, which acknowledged that "the legion was probably not lost in Britain but transferred elsewhere, surviving at least into the mid-120s (on the evidence of the careers of senatorial officers), although suggestions that it perished in the Jewish Revolt, 132-5, or in the Parthian War, 161, are pure speculation".[313] Perhaps "informed speculation" would be more accurate.

---

[313] J.B. Campbell, "Legion", in *The Oxford Classical Dictionary* (4th edn. Oxford 2012), pp. 816-819, at p. 818.

EPILOGUE

PEOPLE LIKE A STORY. However, archaeologists have a duty to base their stories upon the findings of archaeology and upon the suppositions that can legitimately be drawn from these findings. Mommsen erred in straying beyond such reasonable inferences. Collingwood, too. But his narrative was shaped by his particular theory of history. Richmond had no such excuse.

Their fanciful versions of history have had an unfortunate lasting effect. Many writers seem to assume that Mommsen's version of events is still as valid today as it appeared to be in 1885. When we read that "more recent scholarship has tended to reject this theory",[314] it seems as if it is down to personal preference which version of events to accept. Indeed, some appear still to believe that the plot of *The Eagle of the Ninth* is historical fact, such as the writer who recently claimed that "in AD 117 the Ninth Legion was sent to quell some unrest in the area known as Valentia. This legion never returned, and

---

[314] N. Pollard & J. Berry, *The Complete Roman Legions* (London 2012), p. 98.

mystery and speculation surround its disappearance".[315] Others prefer to skate over the complexities of the evidence. Readers of a recent specialist work on the Roman army will find that, while one contributor believes that "Hadrian disbanded *IX Hispana* and *XXII Deiotariana* (or they were destroyed in war)",[316] another can confidently write that "a third legion (*legio VIIII Hispana*) was transferred to Cappadocia, only to be wiped out in a military catastrophe in 161".[317]

Many seem to fall foul of the prosopographical evidence. This was certainly at the root of Richmond's claim that the legion must have been disbanded, as "staff officers at least survived".[318] When Birley drew attention to Lucius Aemilius Karus and Lucius Novius Crispinus as chronologically the last members of the Ninth Legion known to him, his point was that, although both must have served as *tribunus militum* during the reign of Hadrian,[319] they cannot both have been, simultaneously, the tribune on duty on the last day of the legion's existence. Neither, for that matter, did their subsequent car-

---

[315] D. Erb, "The Eagle of the Ninth", in D. Wilson & G.T. Fischer (eds.), *Omnibus I. Biblical and Classical Civilizations* (Lancaster 2005), pp. 535-549, at p. 538.

[316] C. Wolff, "Units: Principate", in Y. Le Bohec (ed.), *The Encyclopedia of the Roman Army* (Oxford & Chichester 2015), Vol. 3, pp. 1037-1049, at p. 1041, while it seems, from Table 8 on p. 1042, that *IX Hispana* remained in Britain only under "Claudius-Domitian".

[317] M.A. Speidel, "Cappadocia", in Y. Le Bohec (ed.), *The Encyclopedia of the Roman Army* (Oxford & Chichester 2015), Vol. 1, pp. 144-146, at p. 145.

[318] See *supra*, pp. 113-114 and 117.

[319] See *supra*, p. 110, for these men.

eers carry the slightest hint that either man had been seriously disgraced.

Nevertheless, even this latter point has recently been contested, in connection with the career of Lucius Novius Crispinus (whom the writer calls 'Saturninus'):[320]

> Here is the intriguing thing – following his posting as a tribune with the 9th Hispana Legion, Saturninus did not receive another official posting for twenty-five years. Only then, after all that time, was he given command of a legion. Normally, after leaving a legion, a man who had served as tribune could be expected to soon take a seat in the Senate and over the succeeding years work his way up the promotional ladder, with a legion command quickly following. After AD 122, Saturninus' career stopped dead. Hadrian would have nothing more to do with him. It was only in AD 147, under the emperor Antoninus Pius, that Saturninus at last received his legion command, that of the 3rd Augusta in Africa. He was by that time aged around 50. A legion commander of that maturity, at any time in Roman history, was rare. Two years later, Antoninus gave Saturninus a new imperial appointment, and his stalled career was on the move again, with a consulship not far off.

---

[320] S. Dando-Collins, *Legions of Rome. The Definitive History of every Imperial Roman Legion* (London 2010), p. 423.

Unfortunately, this summary of Crispinus' career is far from accurate. First of all, he was probably barely into his teens in AD 122, which is far too early for his tribunate.[321] And secondly, we know that he spent his quaestorship attached to the governor of Macedonia, and after his praetorship, he was entrusted with four posts in succession: namely, *legatus Augusti iuridicus Astyriae et Callaeciae* ("imperial legate for the administration of justice in Asturia and Callaecia"), assisting the consular governor of Hispania Tarraconensis; *legatus Augusti legionis I Italicae* (commander of the First Italica Legion), stationed at Novae (near present-day Svishtov in Bulgaria); and proconsul of Gallia Narbonensis; culminating in his Numidian command in AD 147, when he would have been in his late 30s.[322]

Far from languishing "in the official doldrums for a quarter of a century",[323] Crispinus can be seen to have enjoyed a model career under Hadrian and Antoninus Pius. Yet this misreading of his *cursus honorum* has revived interest in Mommsen's version of events, additionally coloured by the plot of *The Eagle of the Ninth* to conjure up "a short, sharp bloodbath [that] surprised and destroyed the 9th Hispana".[324] On the contrary, the answer to the question, "did the legion's second-in-command Lucius Saturninus survive the bloody

---

[321] See *supra*, pp. 79-80.
[322] See *supra*, p. 74.
[323] Dando-Collins, *loc. cit.* (n. 320).
[324] Dando-Collins, *op. cit.* (n. 320), p. 428.

battle and escape back to Roman lines, only to live in shame for the next twenty-five years?", should be an emphatic "no".

Archaeological evidence, by its very nature as the fortuitous survival of the debris of the past, tends not to be abundant. We work with what we have, until the next piece of evidence turns up. New discoveries will surely continue to illuminate the careers of senators like Lucius Novius Crispinus and Quintus Numisius Iunior, bringing us closer to our goal of discovering the fate of the Ninth Legion.

TIMELINE OF EMPERORS

Augustus (27 BC-AD 14)

Tiberius (AD 14-37)

Gaius (Caligula) (AD 37-41)

Claudius (AD 41-54)

Nero (AD 54-68)

Vespasian (AD 69-79)

Titus (AD 79-81)

Domitian (AD 81-96)

Nerva (AD 96-98)

Trajan (AD 98-117)

Hadrian (AD 117-138)

Antoninus Pius (AD 138-161)

Marcus Aurelius (AD 161-180)

Commodus (AD 180-192)

Pertinax (AD 193)

Septimius Severus (AD 193-211)

INDEX

NAMES

Aelianus, L. Roscius, 43-44
Agricola, Cn. Julius, 8, 11, 27, 42, 59, 106
Agrippa, M. Maenius, 105, 116
Alexander, Tib. Julius Julianus, 69
Allectus, emperor, 93
Antoninus Pius, emperor, 54, 55, 56, 58, 62, 99, 127, 139, 142, 143
Apollo Grannus, 127
Arrian(us), L. Flavius, 55-56
Asclepiades, Aelius, 129-131
Augustus, emperor, 7, 22, 34, 38

Babatha archive, 68
Balbus, Q. Flavius, 14
Batavian Revolt, 123
Becker, Wilhelm Adolph, 66
Bertou, Comte Jules de, 61-63, 67
Birley, A.R., 130
Birley, Eric, 114, 116, 117, 118, 120, 127, 133, 134, 136, 138, 141
Blaesus, Q. Junius, 39
Boissard, Jean-Jacques, n.51, 47

Bogaers, Jules E., n.266, 124-125, 129, 131, 138
Boon, George C., 98
Borghesi, Bartolomeo, 50-51, 54-57, 60, 61, 64-67, 69, 74, 80, 81, 82, 118, 135
Boudiccan Revolt, 11, 40, 83
Brigantes, 80, 83, 84-85, 87, 103
Bruce, Revd John Collingwood, 85-87, 105
Brünnow, Rudolf Ernst, 67
Buchanan, John, 94-96
Burbuleius, see Ligarianus
Burckhardt, Jean Louis, 61

Cagnat, René, 4
Camden, William, 84-85, 91, 92
Campanianus, Salvius Nenolaus, 13
Carausius, emperor, 93
Carbuccia, Col. Jean-Luc, 70-71, 72, 73
Carus, see Karus
Cassius Dio, historian, 1, 34, 56, 114, 134
Cerialis, Q. Petillius, 40

Claudius, emperor, 39
Collingwood, R.G., 106, 111-113, 115, 116, 138, 140
Commodus, emperor, 12
Constantius, Caesar, 93
Crispinus, L. Novius, 72-80, 109, 110, 141, 142-144
Crispus, C. Julius Erucianus, 38

Dacian War(s), 45-46, 123, 133
Delamare, A.H.A., 71-72
Dessau, Hermann, 4, 101-102
Dobson, Brian, 116, 127-128
Domaszewski, Alfred von, 13-15, 16, 67, 101-102, 103
Domitian, emperor, 43-46
Drake, Francis, 34

Eck, Werner, 134, 136, 137, 138
Evans, Arthur, 90
Evans, John, 90

Fabretti, Raffaele, 2
Falco, Q. Pompeius, 51
Favorinus, philosopher, 65
Firmus, C. Petillius, 44
Florentinus, L. Aninius Sextius, 62, 64, 66, 67-69, 74, 101-102, 109
Frere, Sheppard S., 119-122, 137-138
Fronto, M. Cornelius, 46, 55, 66, 77-78, 80, 87, 113

Gillam, J.P., 115
Graevius, Johann Georg, 2

Grotefend, Georg Friedrich, 37
Grotefend, Karl Ludwig, 36-40, 42-47, 49, 54, 65, 80, 107, 108
Gruter, Jan, 2, 4, 46, 49

Haalebos, Jan K., n.283
Hadrian, emperor, n.11, n.13, 13, 27, 36, 49, 54-57, 62, 64-67, 69, 74, 78, 83, 84, 87-88, 102, 103-104, 106, 112, 114, 115, 116, 117, 119, 127, 130, 132, 136, 142, 143
Hartley, Brian, 125
Haverfield, Francis, n.173, 86, 96, 102, 106
Henderson, B.W., 103, 106
Henry, Denis, 121
Hensel, Paul and Sebastian, 87
Henzen, Wilhelm, 3, 51, 73-74, 80, 81, 134
Hoare, Richard Colt, 50
Hodgson, Revd John, 89
Horace, poet, 50
Horsley, Revd John, 27-28, 30-31, 34, 49, 86-87
Hübner, Emil, 3, 25, 26, 34, 42, 80, 83, 84, 85, 91, 102
Hull, M.R., 98

Jarrett, Michael G., 116, 132-133, 134
Jewish War, Hadrian's, 114, 129, 131, 134, 138, 139
Joyce, Revd James G., 92-94, 98, 99, 100
Juvenal, poet, 84

Karus, L. Aemilius, 38, 57-60, 69, 109, 110, 141
Kellermann, Olaus, n.106, 81
Kenney, John T., vii
Kenrick, Revd John, 25-26
Keppie, Lawrence, 130-131, 136-137

Laborde, Comte Léon de, 62-63
Laelianus, M. Pontius, 28, 54 n.109
Le Bohec, Yann, 137
Legions
   I *Adiutrix*, 13
   I *Italica*, 45, 143
   I *Minervia*, 45, 123
   I *Parthica*, 48
   II *Adiutrix*, 28
   II *Augusta*, 16, 28, 54
   II *Italica*, 47
   II *Parthica*, 48
   II *Traiana*, 65
   III *Augusta*, 14, 70, 72, 75, 77, 105, 117, 142
   III *Cyrenaica*, 58
   III *Italica*, 47
   III *Parthica*, 48
   IV *Flavia Felix*, 11
   V *Alaudae*, 49
   V *Macedonica*, 13, 45
   VI *Ferrata*, 79
   VI *Victrix*, 28, 35, 49, 54, 106, 108, 112, 113, 123, 128, 133, 136
   VIII *Augusta*, 12
   IX *Hispana*, 30, 34, 37-43, 45, 46, 49, 54, 57, 58, 60, 64, 66, 69, 73, 74, 83, 87, 98, 102-103, 106, 108-110, 111-118, 119-121, 124-131, 132-139, 140-144
   X *Fretensis*, 131
   X *Gemina*, 123
   XI *Claudia*, 13, 45
   XIV *Gemina*, 13, 28, 42 n.85
   XV *Apollinaris*, 17
   XV *Primigenia*, 49
   XVI *Flavia Firma*, 53
   XX *Valeria Victrix*, 28, 45, 54
   XXI *Rapax*, 49, 66
   XXII *Deiotariana*, 49, 66, 141
   XXX *Ulpia Victrix*, 57, 65, 124
Lessert, Clément Pallu de, 75
Ligarianus, L. Burbuleius, 51-57, 59, 61, 109, 110
Linant, Louis, 62
Lipsius, Justus, 46
Long, Henry Lawes, 92

Macer, L. Latinius, 126-128
MacMullen, Ramsay, 1
Malahide, Baron Talbot de, 90
Mann, John C., 129, 132-133, 134
Marcellus, Tib. Teltonius, 14
Marcus Aurelius, emperor, 46, 47, 49, 55, 67, 87, 139
Marliani, Bartolomeo, 47
Marquardt, Joachim, 66-67
Mattingly, Harold, 104
Maximus, Q. Sicinius, 11, 59
Messalinus, C. Ulpius Prastina, 79

Mommsen, Theodor, 3, 50, 81-88, 89, 93, 101, 102, 105, 107, 109, 111, 118, 127, 140, 143

Napoléon III, 74
Natalis, L. Minicius, 12-13
Nepos, T. Haterius, 68
Nero, emperor, 41
Nerva, emperor, 127
Nesselhauf, Herbert, 127-128, 131, 133, 138
Northumberland, 4th Duke of, 91
Numisius Iunior, Q. Camurius, 110, 134-137, 144

Oman, Charles, 103
Orelli(us), Johann Caspar von, 3, 4, 22, 46, 47, 49, 51

Papus, M. Aemilius, 59
Parthian War of Marcus Aurelius, 139
Parthian War, Trajan's, 128-129, 134
Paullinus, C. Suetonius, 12, 40
Percy, see Northumberland
Pfitzner, Wilhelm, 36, 46, 49, 65
Picts, 88
Plarianus, Q. Egrilius, 59
Plautius, A., 39
Pliny (the Younger), 9
Postumus, Poenius, 16

Ramelli, Camillo, 134-135
Renier, Léon, 71-73

Richmond, Ian A., 113, 116-117, 140, 141
Ritterling, Emil, 107-110, 111-112, 114, 118, 136
Rufinus, L. Duccius, 19
Rusticus, L. Antistius, 44
Rusticus, M. Messius, 59

Sabinus, T. Pontius, 105-106, 116
Salway, Peter, 138
Saturninus, L. Martialis, see Crispinus
Saturninus, M. Valerius, 42
Scipio, P. Cornelius Lentulus, 39
Secchi, Giampietro, 61
Septimius Severus, emperor, 48
Severus, M. Cocceius, 127-128
Severus, Sex. Julius, 114-115, 120
Silchester eagle, 93-100
Smetius, Martin, 46
Statianus, T. Caesernius, 78
Steiner, Johann Wilhelm, 64
Sutcliff, Rosemary, vii, 98, 100
Syme, Ronald, n.258

Tacfarinas, 39
Tacitus, historian, 1, 16, 30, 37 n.72, 40, 42, 43
Todd, Malcolm, 138
Tomlin, R.S.O., n.261
Trajan, emperor, 9, 22-24, 36, 44, 45, 55, 57, 59, 64, 65, 66, 67, 76, 83, 102, 106, 109, 113, 123, 127, 133, 138

Varus, P. Quinctilius, 87

Vespasian, emperor, 42, 44
Vindex, C. Vesnius, 12
Vitalis, Tib. Claudius, 44-46
Vitellius, emperor, 41

Watkin, W. Thompson, n.56
Weber, Wilhelm, 103, 106, 107, 109, 111, 116, 119
Wellbeloved, Revd Charles, 20-26, 34, 42, 70
Wellesley, see Wellington
Wellington, 2nd Duke of, 91, 92
Willis, George W., 98
Wilmanns, Gustav, 3, 73
Wissowa, Georg, 107
Wright, R.P., n.267
Yadin, Yigael, 68

Places

Aachen-Burtscheid, 126-127
Africa, 39
Antonine Wall, 88, 95
Aquae Granni, see Aachen-Burtscheid
Arabia, 57, 68
Armenia, 17

Bostra, 14, 62
Brixia, 39
Brohltal, 123

Calleva, see Silchester
Cappadocia, 54-56, 141
Carlisle, 125, 133, 138
Chester, 31
Cilicia, 129-130
Cirta, 78, 79
Colchester, 40
Constantine, see Cirta
Cremona, 42

Dacia, 23, 45
De Holdeurn, 124-126

Diana Veteranorum, see Zana

Eburacum, see York
Elegeia, 34, 134
El-Kasbat, see Gemellae
Exeter, 32

Gallia Narbonensis, 69
Gemellae, 78
Gerasa, 58
Germania, 28, 40, 43, 123-124, 126, 128, 132

Hadrian's Wall, 85-86, 88, 89, 91, 115, 133
Halstatt, 90
Housesteads, 89
Hunerberg, see Nijmegen

Judaea, 58, 121

Lambaesis, 14, 70-72, 74, 75, 77, 78
Lincoln, 40-41

Minturno, 50, 52
Miseno, see Misenum
Misenum, 130
Mons Graupius, 27, 42

Nahal Hever, 68
Naples, 129, 130
Nijmegen, 121, 123-126, 128, 131, 133, 134, 138
Novae, 143
Noviodunum, see Nijmegen
Numidia, 58, 72, 74

Pannonia, 38-39
Petra, 61-64, 67, 68, 69
Pompeii, 92
Rome, 28, 41-42

Scalesceugh, 125, 133

Silchester, 91-93, 95, 96, 97, 98
Stanwix, 125, 133
Svishtov, see Novae

Tazoult-Lambèse, see Lambaesis
Teutoburg Forest, 87-88
Thamugadi, 76-77, 78, 79
Timgad, see Thamugadi

Valenza, 38

Wroxeter, 93

York, 19, 30, 32-33, 42, 71, 83, 84, 87, 102, 106, 107, 121, 125, 128

Zana, 77, 78

INSCRIPTIONS

(All references are to the footnotes)

AE

1890, 75 157	1930, 40 159
1898, 11 152	1940, 220 31
1898, 12 23	1950, 60 162
1902, 146 164	1954, 150 162
1904, 218 168	1968, 323 277
1909, 236 120	1972, 80 288
1910, 161 32	1972, 657 300
1912, 179 30	1975, 446 75
1913, 172 15	1980, 468 91
1925, 126 91	1983, 517 124
1930, 39 162	1984, 529 304

1985, 874 162
1985, 875 167
1987, 414 75
1990, 868 31
1996, 1107 293
1999, 1352 125

2002, 1147 163
2003, 776 81
2004, 1925 121
2011, 204 25
2014, 1657 123
2015, 1904 123

CIL

II, 2424 94
II, 4509 19
III, 87 129
III, 95 24
III, 548 113
III, 6052 32
III, 6755 20
III, 7281 113
III, 14148[10] 140
V, 698 80
V, 4329 79
V, 7443 75
V, 7165 81
VI, 1333 76
VI, 1497 51
VI, 1549 51
VI, 3113 288
VI, 3123 288
VI, 3129 288
VI, 3584 92
VI, 3639 .... 73, 86
VI, 30868 122
VI, 31871 34
VII, 6 195
VII, 7 195
VII, 8 195
VII, 9 195

VII, 184 84
VII, 241 42
VII, 243 35
VII, 445 41
VII, 1224a 59
VII, 1224e 62
VII, 1225c 56
VIII, 2361 162
VIII, 2536 .... 153, 166
VIII, 2542 152
VIII, 2547 155
VIII, 2652 152
VIII, 2666 25
VIII, 2747 149
VIII, 4199 160
VIII, 7036 163
VIII, 10230 165
VIII, 17723 167
VIII, 17849 162
VIII, 17851 164
VIII, 17852 157
VIII, 17860 164
VIII, 17894 158
VIII, 18078 21
VIII, 18214 156
VIII, 18234 156
VIII, 18273 149

IX, 4957 168	X, 6018 104
X, 1769 .... 285, 290	X, 6321 107
X, 3372 288	X, 6928 38
X, 3377 288	XI, 110 288
X, 3402 288	XI, 1834 .... 26, 91
X, 3424 288	XI, 5632 .... 227, 234
X, 3443 288	XI, 6053 17
X, 3445 288	XII, 105 37
X, 3454 288	XIII, 6763 26
X, 3558 288	XIII, 7697 269
X, 3604 288	XIII, 7715 269
X, 3605 288	XIII, 7716 269
X, 3623 288	XIII, 12553 270
X, 3651 288	XIV, 2576 24
X, 3662 288	XIV, 3599 19
X, 3668 288	XIV, 3602 29
X, 4749 26	XIV, 3612 .... 29, 89
X, 5829 ... 228, 230, 234	XIV, 3627 288
X, 6006 .... 104, 105	XVI, app. 13 291
X, 6014 104	

ILS

285 38	1077 76
289 37	1094 51
394 32	1100 51
940 79	1188 26
950 29	2321 75
1000 .... 26, 91	2479 165
1025 .... 29, 89	2656 92
1029 19	2726 228
1035 107	2735 227
1061 19	4449 25
1066 105	5889 80
1068 163	6847 156
1070 149	6850 160

8801	114	9200	34
8834	26	9491	30
9117	32		

RIB

67	195	1091	41
68	195	1427	52
72	195	2462.5	59
87	195	2462.17	62
256	84	2463.4	56
673	35		

Printed in Great Britain
by Amazon